From the L
    David Tidwell

THE MINISTER'S CHURCH,
HOME, AND COMMUNITY
SERVICES HANDBOOK

By James L. Christensen

Funeral Services
The Minister's Service Handbook
The Minister's Marriage Handbook
The Complete Funeral Manual
Contemporary Worship Services
Funeral Services for Today
Don't Waste Your Time in Worship
The Minister's Church, Home,
*   and Community Services Handbook*

THE MINISTER'S CHURCH,
HOME, AND COMMUNITY
SERVICES HANDBOOK

SECTION I

OCCASIONAL HAPPENINGS IN THE LOCAL CHURCH

Service for the Installation of a Minister ... Installation Service for Church Officers ... Installation of Officers of Church Auxiliary Groups ... Recognition of Church Teachers ... On-Site Service of Ground Breaking ... Service of Church Building Dedication ... Celebrating a Church's Mortgage Burning ... Dedication of Church Hymnals ... Dedication of a Sanctuary Organ ... A Budget-Motivation Program ... Consecration Service for Canvassers ... Church-School Promotion Day ... Celebrating the Receiving of a Membership Class Into the Church Family

1

SERVICE FOR THE INSTALLATION OF A SENIOR OR ASSOCIATE MINISTER

Prelude Music

Call to Worship

LEADER "Praise the Lord."

PEOPLE "I will give thanks to the Lord with my whole heart, in the company of the upright, in the congregation" (Psalms 111:1,2).

LEADER "Great is the Lord and greatly to be praised in the city of our God!"

PEOPLE "His holy mountain, beautiful in elevation, is the joy of all the earth, Mount Zion . . . the city of the great King" (48:1,2).

Hymn "Glorious Things of Thee Are Spoken."

Invocation

Eternal God, whose purpose in Creation was revealed in Jesus Christ, who through the centuries has called men to give themselves to establish Thy will on earth and the church to be the redeeming community; bless with Thy Spirit the relationship of church and minister

which has been established through Jesus Christ, who
taught us to pray:

Unison Lord's Prayer and Choral Response

Statement of Purpose

Today this church celebrates an important and decisive milestone in its history. We are gathered to formally install _____ as the minister (*or associate
minister*) of _____ .

Installation Service for Minister

The chairperson of the church (board) will now
bring _____ and (his) family to the chancel.

The Scripture Readings
Old Testament   Isaiah 61:1–3
New Testament   Romans 10:9–15; Matthew 28:18–20

Hymn   "I Love Thy Kingdom, Lord" or "I Love to Tell
the Story"

Sermon   "The Mutual Obligations in Ministry"

Anthem   "How Beautiful Upon the Mountains"
(Harper)

Presentation of the New Minister
CHAIRPERSON OF THE CHURCH (*board*) The church
(board), upon recommendation of the personnel committee has approved the calling of our (brother)
_____ , to the position of

_____. (He) has moved to our city with his family, whom I now wish to introduce to you.
(*Introduction of the individuals of the family.*)
The credentials will be presented by the chairperson of the personnel committee.

Minister's Credentials Read

CHAIRPERSON OF PERSONNEL COMMITTEE (*Here should be presented the family data, educational background, pastoral experience, and notable accomplishments.*)

Ceremony of Installation

CHAIRPERSON OF (ELDERS)   Inasmuch as this sacred act involves mutual obligations, as the chairperson of the (elders) I will call upon you to unite in a covenant of installation. _____, will you stand?

Do you accept the responsibilities of the office to which you have been called, and do you reaffirm your ordination vows, and promise to give yourself wholly to your ministry, to exemplify the life of your Master, and to conduct yourself in such a manner as to reflect credit to Christ and His church?

MINISTER TO BE INSTALLED   Willingly I reaffirm my ordination vows; believing with all my heart that Jesus is the Christ, the Son of the Living God, and accepting the Holy Scriptures as inspired of God through the Holy Spirit, it is my desire to devote my life to the ministry of the Word; so to live as to bring credit and not dishonor to the Gospel which I preach, and to fulfill to my utmost ability the office of a good minister of Jesus Christ. I will diligently and faithfully per-

form all of my duties on behalf of the congregation.[1]
(*Minister may be seated.*)

CHAIRPERSON OF THE BOARD   Will the members of the church (board) please stand and make their commitment.

(BOARD) MEMBERS (*in unison*)   We covenant with God and with our new minister to be loyal to this church and to its head, Jesus Christ, by our consistent attendance, willing service, cooperative spirit, supportive conversation, sacrificial stewardship, and abiding friendship.

CHAIRPERSON OF CONGREGATION   Will the congregation please stand and make your declaration?

MEMBERS (*in unison*)   Affirming our membership in Christ's Church, and our fellowship in this congregation with those of like faith, we renew our vows of fidelity to our Lord Jesus Christ, and our allegiance to His church, solemnly convenanting to work together with our minister to extend the Gospel in its purity and power in this community and throughout the world, and, as faithful servants of the Lord, to give our minister our utmost support in every way, according to our abilities and opportunities.[2]

CHAIRPERSON OF CONGREGATION   Let all remain standing.

Prayer of Installation

Our Father, we pray Thy blessing upon this new minister as (he) assumes the sacred duties with which (he) has been entrusted. Make (his) ministry to be the means of awakening the careless, of strengthening the faithful, of comforting the afflicted, and of edifying the church. Guard (him) against temptation, keep (his) heart pure and steadfast.

Grant to (him) Thy Spirit; Thy love that (he) may win men to Christ; Thy forgiveness that (he) may teach forgiveness; Thy sacrificial Spirit that (he) may go where Thy will directs.

O Lord, bless this congregation, that they may be receptive to leadership and faithful in support. Prepare their minds to receive Thy Word; their hearts to receive Thy love; their wills to receive Thy commission. Sustain them in the bonds of unity; establish them in righteousness; and develop them into Thy community of love; through Jesus Christ, our Lord.

Hymn   "God of Grace and God of Glory"

Benediction

"Let the favor of the Lord our God be upon us, and establish thou the work of our hands . . . yea, the work of our hands establish thou it" (Psalms 90:17). Let Thy loving kindness, O Lord, be upon us.

2

INSTALLATION SERVICE
FOR CHURCH OFFICERS

Executive Committee (*come forward to chancel as name is read*)

Scripture Reading   Ephesians 4:1–3

COVENANT: Do you each accept the office to which you have been selected, and do you promise, the Lord being your helper, to faithfully fulfill its duties?

RESPONSE (*unison*):   I do.

Department Chairmen (*come forward to chancel as name is read)*

Scripture Reading   Ephesians 4:7,11–13

COVENANT: Do you covenant to work together as laborers with God in these specific responsibilities to which you have been appointed?

RESPONSE (*unison*):   I do.

Elders (*come forward to chancel as name is read*)

Scripture Reading   Titus 1:5–9

COVENANT   Do you individually, and in the presence of these people, and before God accept the responsibility of the office to which you have been called by your church?

RESPONSE (*unison*)   I do.

20

Deaconate (*come forward to chancel as name is read*)
Scripture Reading   1 Timothy 3:8–13; Romans 16:1,2
COVENANT   Will you individually and collectively strive as God's helpers to be worthy Christian examples in Christian living and fulfill the responsibilities to which you have been called by this church?
RESPONSE (*unison*)   I do.

Congregation
Scripture Reading   Romans 12:1,2
COVENANT   Will you pledge your eager support to the work of God in this congregation under the leadership of these, your fellow members, who have been elected and selected; and will you renew your vows of fidelity by standing and engaging with me in a common commitment?
RESPONSE (*unison*)   Affirming our membership in the Universal Church and our fellowship in this congregation, we renew our vows of fidelity to our Lord Jesus Christ and solemnly promise that we will work together in brotherly love, as is becoming members of Christ's Church; that we will exercise affectionate care over each other; that we will not forsake the assembling of ourselves together, nor neglect to pray for others; that we will endeavor to win our kindred and acquaintances to the Savior; that we will support the church's work according to our abilities and opportunities, as faithful servants of the Lord, by contributing our time, talents, and money; and we will earnestly seek to live to the glory of Him who has called us out of darkness into light.

Prayer of Installation

Gracious God, who has called men in all ages to be co-workers with Thee in establishing Thy Kingdom on earth; we commend to Thee this church and these officers chosen to lead it. Equip them with Thy Holy Spirit. Make them pure in their motives. Save them from smallness of vision and the temptations to compromise loyalty. Help them to love Christ and His church, to unselfishly dedicate their time, talents, and resources to Christ's Mission.

Grant, our Father, that we may be united as a family, ever seeking to bring others into the fold. Keep us all faithful, until earth's journey shall end, so that we may receive the crown of glory that "fadeth not away," in the promise and love of Jesus. *Amen.*

3

INSTALLATION OF OFFICERS
OF CHURCH AUXILIARY GROUPS

Call to Worship

Lift up your hearts to the Lord. He is the Eternal Father. He is the Redeeming Son. Holy is His life-giving Spirit. With the whole company of heaven and the faithful of earth, we magnify His glorious name, evermore singing:

Hymn   Doxology

Invocation

O God, who art the life-giving presence that makes the trees grow and produce, be also present in our lives, calling us to grow heavenward, to be open to the Son of Man, to grow deep in our faith, and steadfast and unafraid in our serving. Help us to know that we are not alone and isolated. Thy power and wisdom are able to move through us. So we pray that within ourselves, we will let love overcome hatred and prejudice; that within our group and church we will seek the Christian mission and Christian solutions to all problems; that within our nation, we will work to extend human justice and dignity; that within the world, we will wage peace. We yield ourselves as channels of Thy love so that "Thy will may be done on earth as it is in heaven." *Amen.*

The Officers' Charge   (OFFICERS *called by name come to the front*)

To you who have accepted your church and its group's invitation to be an officer, it is my responsibility to remind you that in so doing you become Christ's co-worker and missionary. To be a Christian worker in today's world, one does not let man-made barriers of race, class, or nation separate him from fellow humans. He or she is at home anywhere. Where there is need, you are to seek to be of service. Where there is fragmentation, you are to be God's agent of reconciliation. Where there is injustice, you are to be God's revolutionary

agent for correction. The organization you lead is a part
of the church's mission. You must be diligent in fulfilling your assigned responsibilities for it, so that all who
are confronted by your church and this group may know
God is at work. It will take dedication and sacrifice.

To each one of you, I appoint you as a missionary
witness for Jesus Christ. If you accept, will you light a
candle? "Let your light so shine before men, that they
may see your good works and give glory to your Father
who is in heaven" (Matthew 5:16).

Solo   "One Little Candle" (Roach and Mysels)

Officers' Response in Unison   (*repeat each phrase after*
LEADER)

I will strive/ to live all aspects of my life/ as a testimony to Jesus Christ./ I will strive/ to make my work in
my home/ and outside my home/ in my church and
outside my church/ to be a channel of God's love and
care./ In all of my involvements, I will seek to be a representative of Christ./ I will be creative and dependable
in my service/ as an officer of this Christian group.

The New President

All of us who have been chosen feel the challenge. As
president, I will strive to better understand God's purpose for us as a group. We will need to encourage one
another to face Christ's mission and to find ways to serve
more effectively. Let us respond enthusiastically every
day and in every place. Let us go and live our faith.

RECOGNITION OF CHURCH TEACHERS

Scripture Readings 2 Timothy 2:1,2; Ephesians
4:1–3,7,11–13; Matthew 28:18–20

Purpose

Throughout all history there has been some form of
educational enterprise for sharing the precepts of religious faith. Christianity is rooted in the Judaic tradition of noble teaching. Jesus, the Founder, was a
Master Teacher, who relied upon sharing with and
training His followers. He believed God's Kingdom
could not come until the hearts and minds of men
were prepared for it. Christian teachers stand in the
long procession of men and women who have carried
the light into the world, and communicated the con-
tent of Christ's message from generation to generation.

Because we believe teaching to be a sacred duty and
a primary function for the church, we are here to recognize those choicest souls of this congregation to
whom we have entrusted this responsibility. It is our
desire to express our gratitude for their volunteer service which makes possible our church's educational
ministry.

Presentation of Teachers (THE MINISTER OF EDU-
CATION or EDUCATION CHAIRMAN *calls the names by
departments.* TEACHERS *come to the speaking area.*)

Litany of Appreciation

MINISTER OF EDUCATION   For you whose love and patience, dedication and faith are ever bringing the
dawn of God's new day in and through the lives of
children and youth . . .

CONGREGATION   We express gratitude to God and our
appreciation for your service.

MINISTER OF EDUCATION   For you whose study and
courage are ever guiding and inspiring men and
women in continued spiritual growth and understanding, leading them toward realization of the
Kingdom of God . . .

CONGREGATION   We express thanksgiving to God and
appreciation for your labors.

Presentation of Certificates

MINISTER OF EDUCATION   As a tangible expression of
your church's appreciation and love, we wish to present each of you with a Teachers' Appreciation Certificate, so that you may know that your service has not
been taken for granted.

Charge to Congregation

People can achieve the highest way of life only as they
recognize the relationship they bear to God, and willingly make their wills conform to His eternal will.

Because there are obstacles in the world to increasing

Christlikeness, there must be created a more Christian society, so that personality may reach its highest development.

Because Christian instruction and sharing has to be rooted in a fellowship that is vital and meaningful, it becomes imperative that we sustain our classes in strength. The educational task is so basic that it requires that we give the best of our minds and time, our interest and our inner selves to it.

We challenge the participation and enrollment of every adult, youth, and child of this congregation in some ongoing Christian education class.

Response (*by a* SELECTED TEACHER)

We thank you for these gracious expressions. We acknowledge the sacredness of our task and are humbled by the responsibility to God and to the families of this church. We will strive to train ourselves continually, to prepare prayerfully, to understand those whom we teach, and to provide a worthy example as a pathway to spiritual growth. We need and appreciate your constant encouragement.

Prayer of Consecration (PASTOR)

O Thou Shepherd of the souls of men, who has called these to feed Thy sheep and nurture Thy lambs; bestow Thy favor upon them. They stand in the place of Christ to make Him and His ways known to us and our children. Upon them is the task of interpreting Thy Word, and establishing in the hearts of their pupils a love for all that is divine and eternal. Who can be equal to the task, O Lord? The task is too great, but Thou has promised to Thy teachers, "I am with you always." Fulfill that promise, for the sake of our Great Teacher, Jesus Christ, whose we are and whom we serve. *Amen.*

5

ON-SITE SERVICE OF GROUND BREAKING
(*For Church Building or
Other Church-related Facility*)

Statement of Purpose
We are met here to break the ground out of which shall rise a facility that shall be instrumental to the Kingdom of God.

Fitting is the ancient reminder, "Unless the Lord builds the house, those who build it labor in vain" (Psalms 127:1). Let us therefore lift up our thoughts, voices, and prayers to Almighty God.

Hymn Doxology or "We Would Be Building" or "The Church's One Foundation"

Invocation
Our Heavenly Father, who has revealed the worthy life in Christ and commissioned us to transmit the Good

News; we thank You for the need and the challenge to build that comes to the hearts of us who believe in Christ. As we gather here to break ground for the erection of this facility, unite us in the purpose for which we have been called in Christ, and grant to those who labor here a sense of sacred partnership in the service, for Your Kingdom's sake. *Amen.*

The Scripture Readings
Old Testament   1 Chronicles 29:10–16; 1 Kings 6:1,2, 7,9,11–14
New Testament   1 Corinthians 3:10–17

Brief Homily   (*optional*)

The Litany for Ground Breaking
LEADER   We assemble on this memorable occasion to keep faith with opportunity and with the great crowd of witnesses who have dedicated their time, talent, and substance to the church. We are humbly grateful for all those who have dreamed with us, and to the God of our fathers, who has led us to this place . . .

PEOPLE   We thank You, Heavenly Father, in the name of Jesus Christ.

LEADER   Forasmuch as God has challenged us to erect this (*church or other*) for His glory and the nurture of His people . . .

PEOPLE   We set apart this ground . . .

LEADER   To the glory of God the Father, to the honor of His Son, who loved us and gave Himself up for us,

to the praise of the Holy Spirit, who illuminates and
sanctifies us . . .

PEOPLE   We dedicate this ground.

LEADER   To the construction of this (*church or other*),
where the Word of God will be taught, family life will
be hallowed, children will come to know their Savior,
where young people will be guided and strengthened
for life, where mature persons will find renewal in
mind, body, and soul, where the aging may find comfort and companionship, and the handicapped will
discover joy in living . . .

PEOPLE   We break this ground.

UNISON   We, the members of the _____
Church, in a spirit of gratitude, in the unity of the
faith, in the bond of continuing fellowship, do dedicate ourselves anew to the worship, teaching, and service of Almighty God. We break this ground and set it
apart in the name of the Father, the Son, and the Holy
Spirit. *Amen.*

Presentation of the Architect, Contractor, and Building Chairman

The Act of Ground Breaking   (*Everyone who is present
may be given a small shovel; then outline the perimeter
of the building, and symbolically dig at the given signal;
or, an old-fashioned horse-drawn plow may be used,
with those who desire holding onto one of the lines,
and pulling together to make a furrow; or, selected
OFFICERS may use regular shovels and picks to break
ground. While doing so, the CONGREGATION may sing*

the following, to the tune "Let Us Break Bread Together"):

Let us break ground together, if you please,
Let us break ground together, if you please,
When we push on the shovel with our faces to the rising
    sun,
O Lord, grant mercy to us.

or:

Let us praise God together, as we pull,
Let us praise God together, as we pull,
When we pull on the lines with our faces to the rising
    sun,
O Lord, grant mercy to us.

The Benediction

Now may the blessing of God the Father give diligent oversight to the architect, honest workmanship and freedom from carelessness to those who labor, and faithful support to the members of this congregation throughout this project, in Jesus' Spirit. *Amen.*

6

'SERVICE OF CHURCH BUILDING DEDICATION

Prelude   MARCHE TRIUMPHOLE (Guilmont)

Call to Worship
   "I was glad when they said to me, 'Let us go to the house of the Lord!' " (Psalms 122:1).

Processional Hymn   "God of Our Fathers, Whose Almighty Hand"

Introit

MINISTER   "Give thanks to the Lord, call on his name, make known his deeds among the peoples!"

RESPONSE   "Sing to him, sing praises to him, tell of all his wonderful works!" (Psalms 105:1,2).

CHORAL RESPONSE   "Rejoice Ye Pure in Heart" (*refrain only*)

MINISTER   "We have thought on thy steadfast love, O God, in the midst of thy temple."

RESPONSE   "As thy name, O God, so thy praise reaches to the ends of the earth" (Psalms 48:9,10).

CHORAL RESPONSE   (*Same as above*)

MINISTER   Let us pray.

Unison Prayer

O Lord, our God, exalted above all, of whom the stars sing and whose voice is heard within our hearts; receive our adoration and praise, through Jesus Christ. *Amen.*

Hymn of Praise "All Hail the Power of Jesus' Name" or "The Church's One Foundation"

Reading of the Scriptures Psalms 84:1–5,10–12

Messages of Greetings

The Offering

Doxology

Anthem "All Glory, Laud, and Honor"

Dedicatory Sermon "The Place Where Thy Glory Dwells"

Ceremony of Dedication

MINISTER Having been prospered by our God, and enabled by His grace and power to complete this church building to be used for the glory of His name, we now stand in His holy presence, and dedicate this church. (CONGREGATION *please stand.*) Recognizing our own unworthiness and our reliance upon God for wisdom and strength; conscious of the faith, sacrifices, and love expressed that has made this possible; acknowledging those by whose knowledge, artistic thought and skillful labor this beautiful temple was wrought; remembering all who have loved and served and led this church, especially those who now have joined the Church Triumphant ...

PEOPLE   We, the congregation of this church, dedicate this building to God, our Father, from whom comes every good and perfect gift; to the honor of Jesus Christ our Lord and Savior; to the praise of the Holy Spirit, Source of light and life; and to the work of the whole church.

MINISTER   For the assembling together of the rich and the poor to praise God who is the Master of them all; for the worship of Him in spirit and truth; for the preaching of the Word of God in its fullness; for the administration of the sacraments proclaiming our Lord Jesus Christ as our Savior from sin; for contemplation of beauty, and the experiencing of music ...

PEOPLE   We dedicate this sanctuary to the Lord our God.

MINISTER   For the comfort of those who mourn; for the strength of those who are tempted; for the sanctification of the family; for the building of character; for the giving of hope and courage to all human hearts ...

PEOPLE   We dedicate this chapel to the Lord our God.

MINISTER   To the joy of bread broken together, as Jesus divided with those who loved Him; to the instruction and training of children, youth, and adults; for the development of artistic talents; for the performance of useful service; and to the art of meditation and communion with the unseen and eternal ...

PEOPLE   We dedicate the fellowship hall, the library,

the fine-arts studio, the offices, and the prayer room (*and other*).

MINISTER   As a tribute of gratitude and love, and as an offering of thanksgiving and praise from those who have tasted the cup of Thy salvation and experienced the riches of Thy grace . . .

PEOPLE   We, the people of this church and congregation, now consecrating ourselves anew, dedicate this entire house of the Lord to the worship of Almighty God, and for service to our fellowmen, in the Spirit of Jesus Christ our Lord and Savior.

Dedication Prayer

Almighty God, our Heavenly Father, by whose will and blessings we have built this edifice; now we gratefully dedicate it solely to Thee. We express loving appreciation to Thee for those faithful stewards who have given sacrificially and willingly to make this dream a reality. We express to Thee our appreciation for those skilled craftsmen who have turned timbers and stone into this sacred temple.

For worship, preaching, teaching, and the ministry of comfort in the name of Jesus Christ, and to Thy majestic glory, we set aside this building.

May the favor of the Lord our God be upon us, now and evermore. *Amen.*

Choral Response   (CHILDREN'S CHOIR)

Dedication Hymn   "God of Grace and God of Glory"

Benediction

May the Lord bless your coming in and your going
out, and establish you in every good work and word,
both now and forever. *Amen.*

Postlude   "Festival Toccatu" (Fletcher)

7

CELEBRATING A CHURCH'S
MORTGAGE BURNING[3]

Prelude

Call to Worship

Come, my people, let us give thanks together, for our
God is a generous Father; let us sing together, for our
God is a joyful Father; let us praise together, for our
God is a majestic Father; let us pray and share together,
for our God is a listening and understanding Father.

The Hymn of Praise!   "All Creatures of Our God and
   King" or "Praise to the Lord"

Invocation

Accept our highest praise, as we worship You, O King
of all kings, Lord of all lords, God of all gods. How majestic is Your name in all the earth!

Gloria Patri

The Celebration Invitation

Hymn "Glorious Things of Thee Are Spoken"

The Litany of Appreciation

LEADER Eternal God, for this church facility which has served as our spiritual home for many years ...

PEOPLE We give our thanks.

BUILDING COMMITTEE CHAIRMAN In grateful remembrance of all those who helped prepare this building that it might be fit for serving our people and community ...

PEOPLE We express our gratitude.

LEADER For the services of worship, including baptism and the Lord's Supper, for joyous occasions of weddings, and sad occasions of funerals and memorial services ...

PEOPLE We give our thanks.

BUILDING COMMITTEE CHAIRMAN For lessons taught here by faithful teachers; for special programs and fellowship occasions; for all those influenced to follow Christ as Savior and to walk more closely after Him ...

PEOPLE We give our thanks.

LEADER For all the memories which this house holds for us in our growing awareness of Your presence ...

PEOPLE We give You thanks.

ALL Now in appreciation for the useful functions of this edifice and for an enlarged opportunity of service in the tomorrows, we dedicate ourselves anew to the establishment of Your Kingdom.

Returning the Mortgage

REPRESENTATIVE OF MORTGAGE HOLDER The co-operative efforts of this church and _____(lender)_____ created an opportunity to enhance this growing community. This church and my company (*or bank, other*) entered into this mortgage agreement on _____(date)_____. I happily convey to the people of this congregation the mortgage *now paid in full.*

CHAIRMAN OF BUILDING COMMITTEE As the one honored to serve as chairman of the building committee for this facility, I now receive this mortgage. We can all be proud of the stewardship exercised by all members of the building committee and this congregation, who worked with diligence to complete this obligation. I rejoice with you as I convey to you of this congregation, the mortgage now paid.

CHAIRMAN OF THE BOARD On behalf of all who over the years and who presently have been and are members of this congregation, I receive now this mortgage, shown to be paid-in-full, and offer it now for burning, as an expression of thanksgiving for all who have, through their talents of design and construction, made possible this building; thanksgiving to all who gave oversight to its completion; thanksgiving for the trustees who, by their commitments, made possible the securing of the mortgage, and thanksgiving for the people who through commitments of time, money, and energy have paid the debt on the mortgage. Glory be to God.

Anthem "Hallelujah, Praise the Lord"

The Litany for Burning

LEADER Blessed be the Lord God who does wondrous things.

PEOPLE Being graciously prospered by the hand of our God in lifting the burden of debt from this church of Jesus Christ, we bow, with joy in our hearts, as we transform this cancelled mortgage, the symbol of our completed task, into the incense of prayer and thanksgiving.

CHAIRMAN OF BOARD (*during the building erection*): In love for our church and in reverent memory of all those who by their service and sacrifice have bequeathed to us such valuable and beautiful property . . .

PEOPLE We enter into this service.

PRESENT CHAIRMAN OF THE BOARD With grateful appreciation of the generosity of members, of the fruitful labors of organizations, and of the prayers and labors of the officers of this church . . .

PEOPLE We gratefully share this experience.

LEADER With a prayer that God shall continue to guide us with a spirit of unity and inspire us with wisdom to use our precious heritage, we dedicate ourselves anew to the work of our church for the extension of the Kingdom of Jesus Christ throughout this our community, our nation, and our world . . .

PEOPLE   We now burn this mortgage in the name of the Father, and of the Son, and of the Holy Spirit.

Doxology

The Prayer of Celebration and Thanksgiving

"O Lord our Lord, how majestic is thy name in all the earth" (Psalms 8:1). Here in this place, surrounded by our faith, Thy glory is recognized. From dreams, to convictions, to commitment, to faithfulness, to completion, Thou has led Thy people. We are assembled to rejoice in the victory of joint effort and demonstrated faith.

Many are the hallowed associations this building brings to the minds and hearts of us who are gathered here—of servants who planned, designed, and built these beautiful halls where Thy glory dwells; of devoted ministers who invested their leadership and sacrificed themselves; of generous souls touched by Christ's Spirit, whose faithfulness has paid the obligations; of children and youth and adults whose lives have been enriched and deepened by the activities centered in this place; of those who once stood by our side in this hope, who now are "assembled with the great cloud of witnesses" in the place of their reward.

With hearts attuned in gladness, we rejoice with songs on our lips and prayers in our hearts, thankful for the privilege of being used of Thee and sharing in this victory.

We pledge to Thee an abiding, deep and enlarged service to a new vision, in the name of Jesus. *Amen.*

The Minister's Church, Home, and Community Services Handbook

James L. Christensen

FLEMING H. REVELL COMPANY
OLD TAPPAN   •   NEW JERSEY

Library of Congress Cataloging in Publication Data

Christensen, James L
    The minister's church, home, and community services hand-book.

    Includes bibliographical references and index.
    1. Worship programs.   2. Occasional services.
I. Title.
BV198.C538   264   80-16857
ISBN 0-8007-1128-9

CONTENTS

Introduction

Here is a book to put an end to the minister's frustrations—or a part of them!

What frustrations constantly haunt the Christian minister—primarily because of time limitation! With the demands of the parish, how does today's pastor find time to prepare? The organizational administration takes an increasing and far-too-dominant segment of his schedule. Pastoral duties are forever incomplete and leave him troubled in conscience. The requirements of teaching, preaching, and leading demand preparation—contrary to the common assumption that a minister speaks extemporaneously without meditative study. Whatever the size of congregation he serves, the limitation of time is ever present.

This handbook is designed as a ready resource for the busy pastor, who is also worship leader and pulpiteer. Two sections provide materials for special services, as well as for occasional happenings within the local church. Many of these are not covered by most books of this type.

There are other important occasions in the lives of families that lend to a spiritual dimension, which the wise minister will encourage and utilize. Every pastor frequently is asked to participate or prepare for events in his own community and environs. Herein are helpful resources.

This book balances the traditional language and solid biblical message with the moderate, contemporary mood and style. The result is the kind of handbook that ministers will hopefully find very helpful.

J.L.C.

Hymn   "The Church's One Foundation"

Benediction

May He who has blessed us in our achieving, and thereby called us to new undertakings, be our constant guide toward increasingly fruitful goals, this day and always.

Grace, mercy, and peace be with us, from God the Father and from Jesus Christ the Father's Son in truth and love. *Amen.*

8

DEDICATION OF CHURCH HYMNALS

Prelude

Call to Worship

LEADER   "O sing to the Lord a new song; sing to the Lord, all the earth! Sing to the Lord, bless his name; tell of his salvation from day to day" (Psalms 96:1,2).

PEOPLE   "My heart is ready, O God, my heart is ready! I will sing, I will sing praises! Awake my soul!" (*see* Psalms 108:1).

LEADER   "Make a joyful noise to the Lord, all the lands! Serve the Lord with gladness! Come into his presence with singing! Know that the Lord is God! It is he that made us, and we are his; we are his people, and the sheep of his pasture. Enter his gates with thanksgiving, and his courts with praise! Give thanks to him, bless his name!" (Psalms 100:1–4).

PEOPLE   "I will sing of loyalty and of justice; to thee, O Lord, I will sing" (Psalms 101:1).

Hymn   "Joyful, Joyful We Adore Thee"

Invocation

God of love, who has moved the hearts of people in all ages to adore You, and endowed them with abilities to feel and sing; accept our worship in hymns and spiritual songs. May this collection of hymnody ever be an inspiration to Your church and to Your everlasting glory, in the Spirit of Jesus Christ, the Lord. *Amen.*

Hymnspiration   (*Select a sampling of songs from the new hymnal.*)

The Scripture Lesson   Psalms 104:33; Psalms 92:1–4

The Offering

"With a freewill offering I will sacrifice to thee; I will give thanks to thy name, O LORD, for it is good" (Psalms 54:6).

Choral Anthem   "Renew Thy Church, Her Ministries Restore"

Sermon   "The Glory of Worship"

Litany of Dedication

LEADER   To the worship of God that shall be enriched by the singing of the great hymns of the faith . . .

PEOPLE We dedicate this hymnal.

LEADER To the spirits of the sainted crusaders of the cross, who found in the songs of heroic faith their challenge and their strength . . .

PEOPLE We dedicate this hymnal.

LEADER To the aging and the aged of our church, whose thoughts of God and man through the years have found expression in the songs of faith . . .

PEOPLE We dedicate this hymnal.

LEADER To our Christian youth, whose zealous idealism may be rekindled and renewed by the challenge of song . . .

PEOPLE We dedicate this hymnal.

LEADER To the spirit of unity in the brotherhood of Christians, manifest in the universal singing of hymns by which we may lift a united voice of praise in song . . .

PEOPLE We dedicate this hymnal.

LEADER To the end that our thoughts may be lifted upward in praise, our wills strengthened to do His bidding, and that we may worship the Father in spirit and in truth . . .

PEOPLE We dedicate this hymnal.

Prayer of Dedication

O God, who has given us the gift of music, hearts to love Thee and lips to sing Thy praises; we would praise Thee not with our lips only but with our whole lives. Through the power of song, Thou dost fling open the doors of the heart to worlds unseen where Thou art. We are thankful for creative spirits and interpreters of music, both in the past and the present, by which the visions of the noble life are unlocked. We accept and dedicate these hymnals, grateful for those who made them possible, with the prayer that Thy light may shine on our faces, and Thy love glow within our hearts forevermore, in Jesus' name. *Amen.*

Hymn Response   "Wonderful Words of Life"

Benediction
Bless "one another in psalms and hymns and spiritual songs, singing and making melody to the Lord with all your heart," and the joy of the Lord go with you always (*see* Ephesians 5:19).

9

DEDICATION OF A SANCTUARY ORGAN

Call to Worship
Rejoice in the Lord, O you righteous.

Doxology

The Litany of Dedication
LEADER   "Praise ye the Lord."
PEOPLE   "Praise God in his sanctuary: praise him in the firmament of his power."

LEADER   "Praise him for his mighty acts: praise him according to his excellent greatness."

PEOPLE   "Praise him with the sound of the trumpet: praise him with the psaltery and harp."

LEADER   "Praise him with the timbrel ... praise him with stringed instruments and organs."

PEOPLE   "Praise him upon the loud cymbals: praise him upon the high sounding cymbals. Let every thing that hath breath praise the Lord. Praise ye the Lord" (Psalm 150 KJV).

LEADER   Believing that God has ordained that music be used in the house of worship as an instrument of His praise ...

PEOPLE   We dedicate this organ.

LEADER   For the enhancement of worship for the church, for an appreciation of the music of the masters, and for the development of the language of praise ...

PEOPLE   We dedicate this organ.

LEADER   For beauty in the wedding service, for comfort in sorrow, for thanksgiving on festive occasions ...

PEOPLE   We dedicate this organ.

LEADER   For the healing of life's discords, for the revealing of the hidden soul of harmony, for the lifting of the depressed, for the humbling of the heart before the eternal mysteries of creation, and for the exultation of the soul through noble and transcending melody inspired of God ...

PEOPLE   We dedicate this organ.

The Prayer of Dedication

Father of our Lord Jesus Christ, in whom we live and move and have our being, we magnify Thy holy name.

Jesus our Lord and Savior, Head of the Church and Prince of Peace, we sing praises in Thy name. Holy Spirit of God, our Helper, Guide and Comforter, we lift up our hearts in Thy Spirit. In Thee, all diversity is blended into a matchless symphony of harmony. Thou hast made us to respond to music which is the language of our soul. In song, we are moved in emotion. In words, we hear Thy voice.

So to the communication of Thy peace and harmony to all who worship Thee, we dedicate this organ. Bless thou the ones who play, that they may be sensitive, mature and dedicated Christian musicians. Praise be to Thee, and glory in the Eternal Kingdom, world without end. *Amen.*

Organ Concert

10

THE BUDGET-MOTIVATION BANQUET PROGRAM

(*Cast:* BAILIFF, JUDGE, CLERK, PROSECUTOR, DEFENSE, WITNESSES, AMICUS CURIAE, JURY-CONGREGATION)

THEME: THE CHURCH ON TRIAL

Program Outline

BAILIFF   This Congregational Court will now come to order!

JUDGE   (*swears in* JURY, *on which congregation serves*)

BAILIFF   God's people from (*city or geographical area*) and to the uttermost parts of the world

vs.

_____ Church.

The clerk will now read the Indictment.

CLERK   Comes now the people of _____, of the United States, and even to the uttermost parts of the world on this _____ day of _____, in the Year of our Lord 19____ , alleging and indicting as follows: _____ Church of _____ is organized as a congregation of believers in the Lordship of Jesus Christ, committed to bringing God's Kingdom into this world. To this purpose they

47

regularly have fellowship, purportedly engaging in the winning of souls and carrying out the Great Commission. Notwithstanding the purported high purpose and endeavor expressed by its Constitution and Bylaws, the _____ Church of _____ has willfully, wrongfully, deliberately and selfishly committed the following acts of omission:

First charge   Failure to meet certain basic functions of the church.

Second charge   Failure to strongly support the ministry of the church beyond its own congregation.

Third charge   Failure to give adequate leadership to its young people.

By reason of the willful, wrongful, and selfish acts aforesaid, all of which are in violation of its alleged and pretended purpose and commitment, the _____ Church of _____, has deserted its purpose and commitment, and it should be dissolved and disbanded, its property gathered and sold, and the proceeds distributed to the poor.

JUDGE The prosecution and defense may now make their opening statements.

PROSECUTOR Your honor, we intend to prove the charges as read, which show that this church has neglected the mission to which God called it; we will also prove self-satisfaction, indifference, and unconcern, as well as the inclination to excuse one's own lack of growth by seeing the shortcomings and negligence committed by others.

DEFENSE Your honor, the charges brought are exaggerated. The party charged has shown good faith and should be offered an opportunity to continue and expand its commitment.

Prosecution (*One witness can read several statements or there can be a different witness for each point.*)

PROSECUTOR The first witness will show proof of the First Charge: Failure to meet basic functions of the church.

FIRST WITNESS Very few are concerned about carrying the Word to the unaffiliated in the community—to evangelize or become involved in social action.

SECOND WITNESS They build themselves fancy buildings and bask in their prosperity.

THIRD WITNESS This group has little to offer except for a couple of hours of worship and Sunday school on one morning of the week.

FOURTH WITNESS The men leave the women such key jobs as supporting World Outreach and singing in the choir.

FIFTH WITNESS They wear out the Sunday-school teachers by not training leadership which could relieve them from time to time.

SIXTH WITNESS This church does little to help its members grow in commitment of life; it teaches stewardship only when a new budget comes around.

SEVENTH WITNESS   This church allows its church members to lull themselves asleep without challenging them through vital leadership.

Cross-examination

DEFENSE   You say that there is no concern for evangelism, but isn't it true that _____ persons have been received into our fellowship? Isn't it also true that _____ just recently finished a leadership training class and that other classes will be conducted this spring?

Prosecution

PROSECUTOR   Witnesses will now testify to the Second Charge: Failure to support World Outreach.

FIRST WITNESS   What has this church done to reach the desired goal of appropriation—as much for others as it does for its own local congregation?

SECOND WITNESS   The Outreach budget has been raised in a piecemeal fashion each year.

THIRD WITNESS   This church has never even taken time to seriously consider the challenge facing the church in today's world.

FOURTH WITNESS   Each year the church keeps coming back, asking for more through special days' offerings, such as Christmas, Thanksgiving, Hour of Sharing services.

Cross-examination

DEFENSE   Isn't it true that these special-day offerings are necessary because the pledging commitments are not really sufficient to meet the responsibilities in World Outreach? Also consider the fact that the World Outreach Department seeks to inform the membership through Schools of Missions and Mission Dinners!

Prosecution

PROSECUTOR Witnesses will now testify as to the Third Charge: Failure to give leadership to young people.

FIRST WITNESS This is a congregation of older people—one which leaves young people at the fringes of congregation life.

SECOND WITNESS This church builds great facilities but provides no adequate youth program in it.

Cross-examination

DEFENSE Isn't it true that we baptized _____ young people into the membership of this church? Don't we have leadership from (*name*) and (*name*) and other students?

Prosecution

PROSECUTOR Ladies and Gentlemen, we have presented the evidence which we hope will convince you of the _____ Church's neglect of its mission, its self-satisfaction, indifference, and unconcern.

Defense (*Exhibit* A   *Projected Operational Budget*)

WITNESS We now present the Monthly Treasurer's Report (*as in a regular board meeting*).

Cross-examination

PROSECUTOR We admit that _____ Church has a great heritage and that the current program shows signs of promise for the future, but wouldn't you readily admit that many areas of your program need to be expanded even to approach the needs of God's peoples everywhere?

Defense (*Exhibit* B YOUTH CHOIR)
YOUTH CHOIR (*sings two special numbers*)

Cross-examination (*none*)

Defense (*Exhibit* C *New Building*)
WITNESS We have built a physical plant which would enable us to fulfill our mission in _____ and to be a place of inspiration and learning. It will become a base for service and Outreach.

Cross-examination

PROSECUTOR Don't you agree that such an elegant plant presents a danger that you feel that the job is all done and all your obligations are met?

Defense (*Exhibit* D *The 3-in-1 Program in response to the three charges. Here the Defense will present a comprehensive plan to show the way toward making definite and total commitment of resources.*)

Closing Arguments

PROSECUTOR The urgency of unmet needs must be recognized and dealt with. (*Name them.*)
DEFENSE Progress has been made and more opportuni-

ties to meet these needs will be available. (*Name them.*)

AMICUS CURIAE (*Friend of the Court*)   The true issue is that members need to give for personal growth—growth in Christian stature. Members must assume a plan of sacrificial giving. The church can fulfill its mission, expand its programming, if each member will give adequately. By your pledge, you vote whether the church is guilty or not guilty.

Charge to Jury (CONGREGATION)

JUDGE   Ladies and Gentlemen: The verdict is yours! (*Pledge cards are distributed to each member for his/ her response.*)

11

CONSECRATION SERVICE FOR CANVASSERS

Statement of Purpose

PASTOR   As this congregation is about to enter the intensive week of our campaign for the Program Budget Fund, let us as a congregation and corps of canvassers dedicate ourselves to the obligations and privileges before us.

Charge to the Canvassers

CAMPAIGN CHAIRMAN   You have been selected for the
responsible work of assisting in the Fund Campaign.
You are to go out in the name of Christ and this
church. Your mission is to carry greetings of goodwill
from the church, to talk about the program needs of
our church, and to present the special needs. You are
to contact all families assigned to you. If they are ab-
sent, you are to follow up promptly and receive from
them a definite commitment. You are now hereby
commissioned in the name of Christ to do this important work.

Canvassers' Response

CANVASSERS   As canvassers in the Campaign for our
Program Budget Fund, we accept this charge, and the
responsibility for which we are commissioned. We
promise to lead the way in making our own pledges
first, and to secure the pledges of others. We will do
our best to obtain a definite answer from each member of the church. We will pray daily for the success of
our campaign, that God will use us for His purpose.

Charge to the Congregation

ASSOCIATE PASTOR   You, the congregation of this
church, are asked to pray daily during this coming
week that God will guide you to do your part, according to your ability. We ask that you make your pledge
promptly and cheerfully, remembering that "God
loves a cheerful giver."

Response by Congregation (*unison*)

In grateful recognition of God's gifts to us, we consecrate ourselves and our support, along with our pledges, to the continuing ministry of Christ's church. We dedicate ourselves—and all that we have—as an expression of our Christian stewardship, in honoring God through dedication of time, talent, and possessions. May God's Spirit guide us and use us that His will may be done, and His name be glorified. "Thanks be to God, who gives us the victory through our Lord Jesus Christ" (1 Corinthians 15:57).

Prayer of Dedication

PASTOR   O God, Thou hast been the source of all true life and spiritual attainment in this church. We come as a congregation to answer Thy call to move forward. Stir our hearts with the vision and the zeal to advance Thy work in accordance with Thy will.

We present unto Thee these who have been chosen and who have agreed to visit the congregation in Thy behalf. Thou has used ordinary men and filled them with power for doing the work of Thy Kingdom. Use these men here; endow them with vision to see as Thou dost see, and to have the courage and wisdom to do as Thou would have done. Give them unselfishness, zeal, and may each do his part faithfully and diligently in making Thy Kingdom come on earth. Grant to each member of this congregation receptive hearts and ready wills. Grant us imagination and joy in our giving. Build love among ourselves and devotion to Thee. In the name of Jesus Christ. *Amen.*

12

CHURCH-SCHOOL PROMOTION DAY

(Theme: "Climbing the Ladder." Consideration might be given to carrying out the theme by making "ladder" name tags; students could walk through a large cardboard ladder to receive their certificates.)

PRESIDING: DIRECTOR OF CHURCH SCHOOL

Opening Hymn   "Jacob's Ladder"

Opening Statement   *(by* PASTOR *or* DIRECTOR)
  Today is Promotion Sunday. It is a day when we climb up to another rung on the ladder of spiritual progress. Some will enter into a new department. It is like graduating from one level of achievement to a higher one. It is an experience of great significance. We are here to share the joy of this day and to present symbols of your progress.

Program

DIRECTOR   First let us meet the youngest children to be promoted in our church school. The toddlers will be promoted to the two- and three-year-old class, taught by _____.

LEAD TEACHER OF TWOS AND THREES   Welcome to the two's and three's class! I want to give to each of you a flower with your promotion booklet. (*Calls each one's name as flower is given.*) Flowers speak of love. In your new class, you will learn that "Jesus loves you." Come with me to your new class. (CONGREGATION *hums or sings* "Jacob's Ladder," *as they leave.*)

DIRECTOR   Now our four-year-olds will be promoted to the Kindergarten Department, taught by _____

_____.

LEAD TEACHER OF KINDERGARTEN   Welcome, boys and girls, to the Kindergarten class. My name is _____, and I will be one of your teachers. We want to give each of you a promotion certificate and a picture of Jesus. (*Calls each child's name as picture is given.*) We come to the Church House to learn about Jesus and His people, and to become more like Him. Come with me to your new class. (CONGREGATION *hums or sings* "Jacob's Ladder," *as they leave.*)

DIRECTOR   Now our six-year-olds will be promoted to the Elementary Department, taught by _____ .

ELEMENTARY SUPERINTENDENT   Welcome, boys and girls, to the Elementary Department. My name is _____; I will be one of your teaching friends. We want to give each of you a "Golden Rule Marble."* (*Calls each child's name as marble is given.*) One of Jesus' important teachings was "Do unto

* Marbles may be purchased from Samsonite Corporation, 11200 E. 45th Avenue, Denver, Colorado 80239

others as you would have them do unto you." We will learn what it means to be a follower of Jesus. Come, sit with your new friends of the Elementary Department. (CONGREGATION *hums or sings* "Jacob's Ladder," *as class returns to seats.*)

DIRECTOR   Now our third graders will be promoted to the Junior Department, taught by _____ .

JUNIOR SUPERINTENDENT   As one of the Junior teachers, I am pleased to welcome you. We want to give each of you a promotion certificate and a Bible. (*Calls name of each child, as the Bible is presented.*) The Bible is God's book, for it tells us many wonderful things about God and His love. We will read the Bible and learn how to use it. It is the guidebook to the Christian way of life. Come and be a part of these Junior students. (CONGREGATION *hums or sings* "Jacob's Ladder," *as class returns to seats.*)

DIRECTOR   The sixth-grade class will now be promoted to the Junior-High Department, taught by _____ .

JUNIOR-HIGH SUPERINTENDENT   The Junior-High Department is where we study the courage and manhood of Jesus. He becomes our hero. We welcome you active young people into this department. I present to each of you a certificate of promotion and a cross for you to carry in your pocket. (*Calls name of each youth as cross is presented.***) Jesus died upon the cross. To

---

** Pocket crosses may be purchased from First United Methodist Church, 1928 Ross, Dallas, Texas 75261

be His followers requires sacrifices. In this department we will learn what that means. The cross in your pocket will remind you that you are a follower of the greatest hero the world has ever known. Come and be a part of this fun and exciting group. (CONGREGATION *hums or sings* "Jacob's Ladder," *as class returns to seats.*)

DIRECTOR   The ninth-grade youths will now be promoted to the High-School Young People's Department, taught by _____ .

HIGH-SCHOOL LEAD TEACHER   To feel loved by God and acceptance by our peers is what every young person needs. It is our hope that you who are promoted to this department will find meaningful friendships on the deep basis of life, and will come to know Jesus as a friend to lead you through the most decisive decisions of your life. I welcome you and present to each one a certificate of your advancement and a church hymnal. (*Calls name of each youth as the hymnal is presented.*) The Christian life is one of gladness. The early Christians sang together. Christian young people love to sing, and in this department you will learn the beautiful hymns and choruses of our church. This is just one of the activities of this busy group. Come, join us. (CONGREGATION *hums or sings* "Jacob's Ladder," *as class returns to seats.*)

DIRECTOR   The twelfth-grade youths have now graduated from high-school and will enter the Young Adult Department, taught by _____ .

YOUNG ADULT TEACHER   Though you have graduated,

you are really commencing. You young people are
about to launch into the most challenging and serious
adventure that life holds. Jesus said, "Love the LORD
your God with all your mind, heart, soul, and strength
. . . and your neighbor as yourself." (*See* Luke 10:27.)
To gain knowledge, and then to know how to apply
that knowledge is what education is all about. I am
happy to present each of you a graduation certificate
and a pin. This pin is a lighted lamp, the symbol of
knowledge and wisdom. Paul wrote his young friend,
Timothy, "Study to show thyself approved unto God,
a workman that needeth not to be ashamed, rightly
dividing the word of truth" (*see* 2 Timothy 2:15 KJV).
Accept our invitation to this exciting fellowship.

Closing Statement

May you all continue to grow in the "grace and
knowledge of our Lord Jesus Christ." We trust that you
will be regular in your attendance and diligent in your
study. Have a good year. You are now dismissed to your
classrooms. (*Unison sing* "Jacob's Ladder.")

13

CELEBRATING THE RECEIVING
OF A MEMBERSHIP CLASS
INTO THE CHURCH FAMILY

Minister to Congregation

Dear friends, we are met here to celebrate the initiation of these candidates into the larger family of God's Church. They have met in class to study the meaning of faith and discipleship, and come here to be formally received into this family of God's people. Believing in Jesus as God's Son, they desire fellowship in this church. I ask them to come forward (*read each name*) and in unison to affirm their faith.

The Affirmation of Faith

MINISTER (*asks the* CLASS *standing before him*)   Do you believe in God the Father, infinite in wisdom, goodness, and love; and in Jesus Christ, His Son, our Lord and Savior; and in the Holy Spirit, who takes the things of Christ and reveals them to us?

RESPONSE   I do.

MINISTER   Will you strive to know the will of God, as taught in the Holy Scriptures, and to walk in the ways of the Lord, made known or to be made known to you?

RESPONSE   I will.

MINISTER   Do you confess your sins unto Almighty
God, and putting your trust in Him, promise, in His
strength, to follow His Commandments and to walk
henceforth in His holy ways?

RESPONSE   I do.

MINISTER   Do you seek to yield yourself unto God, that
the same spirit which was in Jesus Christ may be in
you, and that you may be His disciple not in name
only, but in deed and in truth?

RESPONSE   I do.

Prayer
O Lord, bless each of these persons who now becomes
a temple for the dwelling of Your Holy Spirit. *Amen.*

Robing the Candidates (*optional*)

MINISTER   I now put upon you the white robe of purity,
symbolizing the high moral life of Christian discipleship. You are accepted of God. Now are we children
of God; it is not yet made manifest what we shall become. (CLASS *is now seated in special seats near chancel.*)

Reading Words of What God Has Done
Romans 8:1, 2 Corinthians 5:17; Acts 2:38

Homily   "Being Adopted Into God's Family" or "The
Responsibilities of Belonging"

The Welcome

MINISTER *to* CANDIDATES   Will the candidates please
stand and face the congregation?

MINISTER *to* CONGREGATION   Please repeat after me the welcome extended to these new members.

   We welcome you/ into this family/ of God's redeemed community./ You are our adopted brothers and sisters/ in Jesus Christ./ We love you./ We need you./ We encourage you./ Now come to the Lord's Table,/ as guests of Jesus Christ,/ and let us commune together.

MINISTER   The new members may be seated.

Witness of the Community of Faith
   1 Peter 2:9,10; Galatians 3:26–28; Ephesians 2:19; 5:1

Prayer of Thanksgiving
   For the new family relationship in the Church of Jesus Christ, we are grateful; and for the life of these with whom we are bound in Jesus Christ. As we eat of this supper, bless the mystical ties that make us one in Christ. *Amen.*

Distribution of Emblems
MINISTER   Please hold emblems for simultaneous participation. (NEW MEMBERS *of church family served first; then the entire* CONGREGATION; *or the* CONGREGATION *may come forward in a circle surrounding the* MEMBERS.)

Words of Institution
   We now belong to one another because we belong to Christ. This is the family gathering. The Lord Jesus took bread, He gave thanks, broke it and said, "This is my body, which is for you. Do this in remembrance of me. . . ." (CONGREGATION *eats bread.*) He did the same

with the cup. He said, "This cup is the new covenant in my blood. Every time you drink it, do it to remember me." (*See* 1 Corinthians 11:25; *the* CONGREGATION *takes the cup.*)

Hymn   "Blest Be the Tie That Binds"

Benediction

"Now to him who is able to keep you from falling and to present you without blemish before the presence of his glory with rejoicing, to the only God, our Savior through Jesus Christ our Lord, be glory, majesty, dominion, and authority, before all time and now and for ever. Amen." (Jude 24, 25).

Passing of the Peace

MINISTER   Each member of the congregation will come by the newly initiated, cover (his) hands with (his) own, and say, "_____ (name), the peace and joy of God be with you."

SECTION II

SPECIAL-DAY SERVICES
FOR THE LOCAL CHURCH

Advent Celebration Service ... Advent Sundays ... Christmas Service of Carols and Candles ... Lenten Season Material ... Holy Week Resource Material (Palm Sunday, Maundy Thursday, Good Friday, Easter) ... Easter Service of Worship ... Pentecost ... Worldwide Communion Service

14

ADVENT CELEBRATION SERVICE

Prelude Music   "Sleepers Awake" (Bach)

Processional Music   "Love Divine, All Love Excel-ling" (*The* CHOIR's *processional should have a joyous step. They should go down the aisle; divide into single lines in front of the pews; then back the side aisles toward the entrance; again down the center aisle; thence to the chancel area or wherever the* CHOIR *is to be located.*)

The Affirmation of Joy

LEADER   Friends, we are here to celebrate Good News! It has come from God into the world! The whole human prospect has changed since God invaded our life in Jesus of Nazareth!

PEOPLE   Oh, what joy fills our hearts! Glory be to God!

CHOIR   Noel, Noel, Noel! (*Sing triumphantly from the Introduction to the* "Shepherd's Story" *by Clarence Dickinson, first line only.*)

LEADER   Friends, to celebrate the Advent requires preparation, as John pleaded long ago, "Prepare a road for the Lord. Straighten out the path where He will walk."

PEOPLE   Come, Lord Jesus! Every crooked way shall be made straight. Every knee shall bend, and every tongue shall confess You to be the Lord of heaven and earth. Rejoice.

CHOIR   *(second line only; see above)*

Invocation Prayer

The heavens rejoice and all the earth is glad, O God, because You have invaded the world in Jesus Christ, and through Him are perfecting and completing all creation, casting out all darkness with Your pure light, bearing the burdens and sins, preparing the kingdoms of the world to become Your Kingdom, world without end. So may it be. *Amen.*

CHOIR *Response   Gloria in Excelsis*

Anthem   "Glory to God in the Highest" (Pergolesi)

The Reading of the Word

From the Old Testament   Isaiah 9:2–7; or Isaiah 55:6–15 (LB).

CHOIR *and* CONGREGATION *Response*   "Let All Mortal Flesh" *(verse 1)*

From the New Testament   John 1:1–14; or 1 John 1:1–10

CHOIR *and* CONGREGATION *Response*   "Let All Mortal Flesh" *(verse 2)*

The Now Reading[4]

What in the world is the meaning of this?

In the beginning was the Word, divine, distant, indescribable, unspeakable.

In the beginning was the Word unrevealed, mysterious, transcendent.

And the Word became flesh, and dwelled among us,

defining the undefinable, speaking the unspeakable, actualizing the incredible.

Out of the all of everything the Word became Someone, Someone in particular.

But Someone in finite form, in plain-as-day flesh.

The Word became flesh, so that men of flesh could see, hear, touch the reality of the Word.

The Word had always been present, yet hidden in the folds of life, but man's eyesight was weak and his insight weaker.

So the Word became flesh that men might see, hear, touch, know, and experience the Word.

The Incarnation, the en-flesh-ment of the Word, was not just a communication technique.

It goes deeper than that.

The Word became flesh because it is the nature of the Word to enter, invade, to be where the action is.

The Word became flesh because it could not and, in the present tense, cannot remain unattached, uninvolved, uncommunicated.

The Incarnation was a once-in-history visible illustration of the Word's continuous presence in the world.

The Incarnation event *à la* Jesus of Nazareth happened once, but the reality it revealed is always happening.

Just as there were many in that day who saw but did not see, so, in our day, we must see and perceive the ways in which the Word is continually "in our midst."

The Word came to live through the Someone of flesh,

and the Word came alive to those who saw, heard, touched, experienced the Word.

And the Word comes alive to us in our present, tense times.

Recognize Him; give Him room, and a place to stay till the Word indwells your flesh.

CHOIR *and* CONGREGATION *Response*   "Let All Mortal Flesh" (*verse 3*)

The Advent Prayer

Hidden God, wherever You are in Your kind of space; You will have to take the initiative to break through to reach us. We keep throwing up roadblocks of doubt, smoke screens of laziness, and endless ingenious excuses. Break through this heavy human wall with the blast of an embryo. Break through and join us—become one of us and shock us with Your Son. Yes, shock us. We need it. *Amen.*

The Offering and Doxology

The Anthem   "O Come, O Come Emmanuel"

Sermon   "Christ . . . In the Most Unlikely Places"

Hymn   "What Child Is This?"

Closing

"A king might miss the guiding star, a wise man's foot might stumble; for Bethlehem is very far from all except the humble" (Louis F. Benson).

Only the childlike in spirit have the capacity to receive the Lord of glory, who came to earth as a child.

Benediction

May the King Eternal, who surprised the world long ago, not go unrecognized today as He makes His visitation. May the Holy Spirit prepare your hearts to discern Him, to receive Him, and to give to Him, now and forever. *Amen.*

15

ADVENT SUNDAYS

THE FIRST SUNDAY IN ADVENT:

Lighting of First Advent Candle

LEADER   The first candle on the Advent Wreath has been called the *Prophecy Candle,* opening the four-week period of waiting for the birthday celebration of Christ. As a representative of the congregation, the _____ family will light the first candle.

PEOPLE   The prophet Isaiah prophesied, "Behold, darkness shall cover the earth ... but the Lord will arise upon you.... and the people who walked in darkness [shall see] a great light" (Isaiah 60:2; 9:2).

LEADER   The promise has been fulfilled. "There shall
   come forth a shoot from the stump of Jesse, and a
   branch shall grow out of his roots . . . the spirit of wisdom and understanding, the spirit of counsel and
   might, the spirit of knowledge and the fear of the
   Lord." (11:1,2).

PEOPLE   We light the flame of hope in our hearts.

Unison Prayer

O Lord our God, who has given light to shine out in
darkness, and has awakened us to praise Your goodness;
accept our expressions of thanksgiving. Direct us from
the bitter darkness of our misdeeds, and grant us Your
good Spirit, that we may become children of light and
inheritors of the promise fulfilled in Jesus Christ. *Amen.*

Suggested Hymns   "O Come, O Come Emmanuel";
   "Come, Thou Long-Expected Jesus"; "There's a Song
   in the Air"; "Lo, How a Rose E'er Blooming"

Suggested Scripture Readings

From the Psalms   89:19–22,24; 96

Old Testament Lessons   Jeremiah 23:5,6; Micah
5:2–4

New Testament Lessons   Luke 1:26–33; 1 John 1:1–10

Pastoral Prayer

Eternal God, who broke into our human life deci-
sively in Jesus Christ; accept our grateful praise. For
Thy rich redemption, dimly dreamed, long promised,
earnestly desired, and at last experienced in Jesus, we
are humbly indebted.

We are thankful for all prophetic spirits who believed

the promise of a better day and by faith served it. We are thankful for the faithful men and women who, even in days of discouragement, believed in Thy goodness, and in the nights of darkness watched for the morning and trusted in the coming dawn. We pray today for a vision of our Redeemer, for a like faith, and the unflagging zeal to follow faithfully the Star of Hope.

May this Advent season deepen our trust in Thee. May the Spirit of Christ come more and more into our life. Hasten the day when men everywhere shall rejoice in the Good News of peace on earth, goodwill toward men. Enable us to do all that we can to make Christ known and loved, and served for Thy Kingdom's sake. *Amen.*

Offertory Sentence

"What shall I render to the Lord for all his bounty to me? I will lift up the cup of salvation and call on the name of the Lord. I will pay my vows to the Lord in the presence of all his people" (Psalms 116:12–14).

Offertory Prayer

Gracious God, who has richly blessed us, how can we ever deserve Thy mercy? We cannot pay our debt of gratitude; we can only bring expressions of our love. We do not bring that which costs us nothing, but living sacrifices of dedicated lives for honoring Jesus Christ. *Amen.*

Suggested Anthem "Good News From Heaven" (Bach)

Closing Hymn "Lift Up Your Heads, Ye Mighty Gates"

Benediction

May the power of the Most High, the lowliness of Jesus Christ, and the overshadowing of the Holy Spirit, give you peace, and love, and everlasting joy. *Amen.*

THE SECOND SUNDAY IN ADVENT:

Lighting of Second Advent Candle

LEADER   The second candle on the Advent Wreath has been called the *Bethlehem Candle,* a symbol of the preparation being made to receive and cradle the Christ Child. As a representative of the congregation, the ＿＿＿＿＿＿ family will light the first and second candles.

PEOPLE   As it is written in the Book of Isaiah, "Listen, I hear the voice of someone shouting. 'Make a road for the Lord through the wilderness; make him a straight, smooth road through the desert. Fill the valleys; level the hills; straighten out the crooked paths and smooth off the rough spots in the road. The glory of the Lord will be seen by all mankind together' " (Isaiah 40:3–5 LB).

LEADER   Today we are preparing for Christmas in various ways—cards, gifts, decorations, lights. The most important preparation seems to be personal and social.

PEOPLE   "And the glory of the Lord shall be revealed, and all flesh shall see it together, for the mouth of the Lord has spoken." (40:5 RSV).

Unison Prayer
Almighty God, who prepared the world of old for the life and ministry of Jesus, prepare now our minds and hearts to receive the fullness of Thy blessing in Jesus Christ our Lord. *Amen.*

Suggested Hymns "Come Thou Long-Expected Jesus"; "Let all Mortal Flesh Keep Silence"; "Hush, All Ye Sounds of War"; "Lift Up Your Heads, Ye Mighty Gates"; "It Came Upon the Midnight Clear"

Suggested Scripture Readings
From the Psalms   24:3–10; 72:18, 19
Old Testament Lesson   Isaiah 11:1–10; 42:1–4
New Testament Lesson   Matthew 2:1–3; 25:1–13; Romans 13:8–14

Pastoral Prayer
Merciful God, we acknowledge before Thee our deep need of Christ's Spirit in our hearts. We confess our own share in the selfishness which rules in human life; in the prejudices and suspicions which divide men; in the love of unworthy things which cheapens life; in the timidity which holds back good causes; and in the indifference which allows evils to go unchecked. We confess our broken vows of loyalty to Christ; our obedience to the powers of evil which He hates; our lack of faith in the way of love which He leads.

Forgive us, our Father. We thank Thee for Thy patience, which puts up with our folly, but we rejoice that Thy faithfulness ever seeks to save us from our foolishness. We are overawed by the assurance that when we turn to Thee, Thou hast already turned to us. May the mystery of Thy love indwell us, so that we may be saved from false pursuits, hardened spirits, and vain ambitions. Prepare our lives for Jesus' entrance.

In this Advent season, may old enmities be laid aside and ancient feuds be terminated; may hardened grudges melt from the heart and bitterness be wiped out by the remembrance of Thy forgiveness. May the prodigal come back to the family circle and the Father's forgiveness. Help us all to put away all untruthfulness and greed, all malice and cowardice. May Thy Holy Spirit cleanse us from our sins and teach us to love one another, even as Thou dost love us, through Jesus Christ. *Amen.*

Offertory Sentence

Remember the words of our Lord Jesus who said, "It is more blessed to give than to receive" (Acts 20:35).

Offertory Prayer

O Lord, forgive us for acting as though our ease, comfort, and wealth has been of our own making. Forgive us for confusing our material wants with our actual needs. Forgive us who have so much for thoughtlessly ignoring those who have so little. Inspired by the example of Jesus, we bring to Thee our offerings of love and sacrifice to honor Thy holy name. *Amen.*

Suggested Anthem
"Glory to God in the Highest" (Pergolesi)

Suggested Closing Hymns
"Watchman! Tell Us of the Night"; "Wake, Awake, for Night Is Flying"

Benediction
"Grace be with all who love our Lord Jesus Christ with love undying" (Ephesians 6:24).

THE THIRD SUNDAY IN ADVENT:

Lighting of the Third Advent Candle

LEADER   The third candle is the *Shepherd's Candle*. It represents the sharing of Christ's love. Representing the congregation in the lighting is the _____ family.

PEOPLE   We are halfway in our preparation for celebrating the Christ event which changed forever the human outlook. As we worship today, we bring our gifts of food and money to make others happy; thus we share the love of Jesus Christ.

LEADER   "How beautiful upon the mountains are the feet of him who brings good tidings, who publishes peace, who brings good tidings of good, who publishes salvation" (Isaiah 52:7).

PEOPLE   "Let your light so shine before men, that they may see your good works and give glory to your Father" (Matthew 5:16).

Unison Prayer

Gracious Father God, we rejoice in Thy love shown to us in Jesus Christ. In response to Thy loving kindness, we worship Thee and joyfully share with others in the Spirit of Jesus Christ our Lord. *Amen.*

Suggested Hymns "Angels We Have Heard On High"; "We Three Kings"; "Angels From the Realms of Glory"; "The First Noel"

Suggested Scripture Readings
From the Psalms 100 or 98
Old Testament Lesson Isaiah 55:1–9
New Testament Lesson John 1:1–18

Pastoral Prayer

God Almighty, we thank Thee for humbling Thyself to share our common life, to dwell in the midst of humanity, to endure the bitterness and cruelty of our nature to effect our deliverance. Because Thou has first loved us, we would love others.

At this season, when we celebrate Thy Incarnation, each Christmas gift is a reminder of hearts made tender and unselfish by Thy generosity. Every deed of kindness is evidence of Thy Spirit alive in our world. Every child reminds us of the qualities that inherit Thy Kingdom. The Christmas sharing brings to memory our Lord's pity for the poor and the oppressed, and how compassionate He was with them.

Grant, O Lord, that the season may trigger such an outpouring of generous sharing that the light of Christ's compassion may be experienced. Bless with Christian concern the sick and sorrowful, the distressed and broken, the lonely and disheartened. May no one be forgotten or uncared for this season. Out of the turmoil of the world's sinful darkness, may the light of brotherhood and peace shine from Him who is our Lord, Jesus Christ. *Amen.*

Offertory Sentence

"I was hungry and you gave me food, I was thirsty and you gave me drink, I was a stranger and you welcomed me, I was naked and you clothed me, I was sick and you visited me. . . . Truly, I say to you, as you did it to one of the least of these my brethren, you did it to me" (Matthew 25:35,36,40).

Offertory Prayer

O Lord, we dedicate these offerings and pray that in Thy Spirit the ministry of compassion may be multiplied in feeding the dispossessed, sharing with the needy, healing the brokenhearted, and uniting us in human concern. Sanctify our gifts and glorify Thy Son our Savior, through our humble service. *Amen.*

Suggested Anthem "A Carol From Midwinter" (Milford)

Suggested Closing Hymns "Lo, He Comes"; "On Jordan's Bank the Baptist's Cry"

Benediction

"May the God of peace himself sanctify you wholly; and may your spirit and soul and body be kept sound and blameless at the coming of our Lord Jesus Christ" (1 Thessalonians 5:23).

THE FOURTH SUNDAY IN ADVENT:

Lighting of the Fourth Advent Candle

LEADER   The fourth candle is the *Angel's Candle,* the candle of love and final coming. The same God who said, "Out of darkness let light shine," has caused His light to shine upon us, around us, and in us to give the revelation. His light is fully ablaze. Representing the congregation in the lighting is the _____ family.

PEOPLE   Jesus is the Light of the world. He comes to bring us light that illumines God; light that reveals life's meaning; light that penetrates the future; and light that makes plain the holy purpose.

LEADER   God is Light, and in Him there is no darkness at all. If we walk in the light as He is in the light, then we share together a common hope and are being cleansed from every sin.

PEOPLE   Glory be to God.

Unison Prayer

Everlasting God and Father, who art the Star of Hope and the Desire of All Nations; the world is full of Thy glory. We praise Thy holy name and earnestly pray that Thy radiant light will penetrate people's hearts everywhere with warmth and truth, reigning in our affections as the King of Love, and in the world to dispel crime and war as the Prince of Peace forever. *Amen.*

Suggested Hymns "Joy to the World"; "O Come, All Ye Faithful"; "Good Christian Men, Rejoice"; "Angels, From the Realm of Glory"; "O Little Town of Bethlehem"

Suggested Scriptures

From the Psalms 72;150

Old Testament Lesson Isaiah 9:2–7; 40:1–11; 55:1–9

New Testament Lessons Matthew 2:1–12; Luke 2:1–20

Pastoral Prayer[5]

O Christ, whose star led the Wise Men and the shepherds to Thy side on that momentous night in Bethlehem, lead us again to Thy side. Even as did the shepherds kneel in awe and wonder at the announcement of Thy birth, may we humbly bow our hearts in reverence to Thee. We would come to bring Thee ourselves, that we might become Thy followers and Thy disciples in all of our living.

O Thou Light of Bethlehem, let the light again shine upon a world so ill at ease. Let again the angel voices speak peace to a turbulent world. Let Thy Spirit calm the unrest.

We thank Thee, Thou Child of Bethlehem, whose names were foretold in prophecy: Wonderful, Counselor, Mighty God, Everlasting Father, Prince of Peace—that Thou art worthy of those titles. We would that they might be lifted up as banners over our world.

Help us to know the meaning of love to God. Help us to make it supreme. Guide us to greater patience and temper our desires with sacrifice. In His name we pray. *Amen.*

Offertory Sentences
"When they saw the star, they rejoiced exceedingly with great joy; and going into the house they saw the child with Mary his mother, and fell down and worshiped him. Then, opening their treasures, they offered him gifts, gold and frankincense and myrrh" (Matthew 2:10,11).

Offertory Prayer
Not of our deserving, but of Thy mercy, we have been blessed with the gift of Jesus Christ. In response to Thy love, we bring our treasures: the fine gold of obedience, the fragrant incense of prayer, and the healing myrrh of devotion. Remembering our accountability to Thee for the use we make of our time, talent, and money, we pray that they may reflect responsible stewardship and be acceptable to Thee. *Amen.*

Suggested Anthem   "Good Christian Men, Rejoice" (Whitehead)

Suggested Closing Hymns   "The First Noel"; "Hark! The Herald Angels Sing"

Benediction
Send us forth, O God, with clear, unshakable purpose and with contagious joy to do our part in building upon the earth Thy Kingdom, in Jesus' name. *Amen.*

16

CHRISTMAS SERVICE OF
CAROLS AND CANDLES

Preparation for Worship (*Instrumental music: violin, harp, trumpet, and so forth*)

Choral Call to Worship

Opening Hymn "Joy to the World"

Call to Worship

"The angel said, 'Behold, I bring you good tidings of great joy, which shall be to all people. For unto you is born this day in the city of David, a Saviour, which is Christ the Lord. . . . Thanks be unto God for his unspeakable gift' " (Luke 2:10; 2 Corinthians 9:15 KJV).

Invocation

Our God and Father, we come to Thee rejoicing in the gift of Thy Son to the world. We turn our thoughts toward the birth of Jesus Christ who brought light into the world. Bless us, as in our worship we travel again to Bethlehem and pray as Jesus taught us:

Unison Lord's Prayer

Choral Response

THE PROMISE OF THE LIGHT OF THE WORLD

His Coming Foretold   Isaiah 9:2–7

A Carol   "It Came Upon the Midnight Clear"

THE PREPARATION FOR HIS COMING

The Annunciation   Luke 1:26–33

A Carol   "What Child Is This?"

The Offering

Anthem   "Let Our Gladness Have No End" (Neske); or "Holy Night" (Adam)

Carol   "We Three Kings" (*as offering is brought to chancel*)

Dedication Prayer for Christmas Offering:

O Lord of light and life, as of old, men came from watching in their fields, and kings from their dominions to behold the Savior born in a manger; so we come from our various fields of work to worship Thee. Bless these gifts that we bring, so that the light of hope and peace may shine in power over the entire world, through Jesus Christ, *Amen.*

THE COMING OF THE CHRIST CHILD

The Fulfillment of the Promise   Luke 2:1–17

Solo   "The Birthday of the King"

The Christmas Sermon   "God's Unspeakable Gift"

Carol   "O Little Town of Bethlehem"

THE SERVICE OF LIGHTS

Communion Prayer

FOR THE BREAD   We praise thee, O God, and bless Thy holy name, because Thou hast not withheld Thy mercy from our sinful race; but in the fulness of time humbled Thyself in the Incarnation and gave Thyself in the Crucifixion that we might receive adoption and eternal salvation. Bless this sacred bread that we eat so that Jesus Christ may invade our being, for Thy name's sake. *Amen.*

FOR THE CUP   O God, we bow in adoration for the Christ Child, who grew up to become a Man of spotless humanity, tender charity, spiritual power, amazing love, and faithfulness unto death. Grant us to receive of His fulness and grace, so that we might experience the turning on of light within, which comes from the Spirit of the indwelling Christ. Then so perfect us in His likeness, that we may be lights in the dark world and experience at last His triumph and glory in heaven. *Amen.*

Choir   "One Little Candle" (Roach and Mysels)

Communion Participation

Please come forward to serve yourself; then take a candle, light it, and form a large circle around the sanctuary.

Carol   "Silent Night"

Christmas Blessing[6]

Blessed are you who find Christmas in the age-old story of a babe born in Bethlehem.

   To you a little child will always mean hope and promise to a troubled world.

Blessed are you who find Christmas in the joy of gifts sent lovingly to others.

   You shall share the gladness and joy of the shepherds and wise men of old.

Blessed are you who find Christmas in the fragrant greens, the cheerful holly, and soft flicker of candles.

   To you shall come bright memories of love and happiness.

Blessed are you who find Christmas in the Christmas star.

   Your lives may ever reflect its beauty and light.

Blessed are you who find Christmas in the happy music of Christmastime.

   You shall have a song of joy ever singing in your heart.

Blessed are you who find Christmas in the message of the Prince of Peace.

   You will ever strive to help Him bring peace on earth, goodwill to men.

Benediction

While you are placed among the things that are passing away into darkness, may you ever cling to those that shall abide in Jesus Christ. Let your light shine before men to illumine the darkness. God bless you everyone. *Amen.*

Postlude "Christmas Morn" (Handel)

17

LENTEN SEASON MATERIAL

Calls to Worship

"The sacrifice acceptable to God is a broken spirit; a broken and contrite heart, O God, thou wilt not despise" (Psalms 51:17). "Humble yourselves before the Lord and he will exalt you. Draw near to God and he will draw near to you. Cleanse your hands ... and purify your hearts" (James 4:10,8).

or:

"Come now, and let us reason together, saith the Lord: though your sins be as scarlet, they shall be as white as snow; though they are red like crimson, they shall be as wool" (Isaiah 1:18 KJV).

Invocation

Father of our everlasting hope, whose Son Jesus Christ suffered on the cross; help us to meet the cares and sufferings of daily life with faith and patience. We ask not for any prosperity that would tempt us to forget Thee. As disciples of One who had no place to lay His head, we seek only the strength to glorify the cross.

Suggested Scripture Reading:
From the Psalms 143; 39; 32; 130
Old Testament Lessons Exodus 20:1–20; Jonah 3; Isaiah 1:1–20; Genesis 9:1–14
New Testament Lessons Luke 4:1–13; John 6:27–35; Mark 10:32–45; Luke 15:11–24

Suggested Hymns "Lead On, O King Eternal"; "Rejoice Ye Pure in Heart"; "The Son of God Goes Forth to War"; "Beneath the Cross"; "O Love That Wilt Not Let Me Go"

Pastoral Prayer
O God, eternal love; in the shadow of the cross, we worship and bow down, subdued by a mystery beyond our fathoming, and awed by a love greater than our hearts. When we think of Jesus, we are melted by an unutterable tenderness.

During this Lenten period, we pray for the desire and courage to deny ourselves, inspired by Jesus Christ.

O Lord, deny us of anger, so that we may know the meaning of self-control.

Deny us of gossip, so that we may know the meaning of thoughtfulness.

Deny us of stinginess, so that we may know the meaning of generosity.

Deny us of pettiness, so that we may know the meaning of greatheartedness.

Deny us of faultfinding, so that we may know the meaning of friendship.

Deny us of self-righteousness, so that we may know the meaning of humility and repentance.

In denial, dear Jesus, may we be taught and trained for higher service in Thy Kingdom, for Thy name's sake. *Amen.*

Offertory Sentence

Jesus said, "If any man would come after me, let him deny himself and take up his cross [daily] and follow me" (Matthew 16:24).

Offertory Prayer

O Christ of God, who once said, "For their sake I consecrate myself" (John 17:19), then followed it with action and sacrifice upon the cross; grant us such a measure of Thy Spirit that we may forget ourselves in concern for others, and never shrink from sacrifice. Forbid that we should complain about burdens that are not worth comparing with the sufferings of Jesus. Accept our offerings, and may they be used to help the sick, the hungry, and the lonely in Jesus' Spirit. *Amen.*

Suggested Anthem "Behold the Lamb of God" (Handel); or "All We Like Sheep Have Gone Astray" (Handel)

Suggested Closing Hymns "Lead On, O King Eternal"; "My Faith Looks Up to Thee"

Benediction

"The grace of the Lord Jesus Christ and the love of God and the fellowship of the Holy Spirit be with you all" (2 Corinthians 13:14).

18

HOLY WEEK RESOURCE MATERIAL

PALM SUNDAY

Call to Worship

"Lift up your heads, O gates! and be lifted up, O ancient doors! that the King of glory may come in.... Who is this King of glory? The Lord of hosts, he is the King of glory!" (Psalms 24:7,10).

The voice of rejoicing and salvation is in the tabernacles of the righteous. Blessed is He that comes in the name of the Lord.

Invocation

God of truth and righteousness, we praise Thee for the Master who rode in triumph into the city of His fathers to challenge their evils. We thank Thee that Jesus came, not as a conqueror to destroy, but as a Messiah to save. In the spirit of praise and reverence, we bow and

with our tongues confess that Jesus Christ is Lord, to
Thy glory, O God, our Father. *Amen.*

Palm Sunday Litany[7]

LEADER   Our Father, we take our place among the glad
multitude who hail the King of kings. Stir us and our
complacent nation anew because of His coming.

PEOPLE   Blessed is He that cometh in the name of the
Lord.

LEADER   O God, whose dearly beloved Son was greeted
by the crowd with *hallelujahs,* but who later that same
week was mocked, as He followed His lonely way to
the cross; forbid that our welcome to Him should be
in words alone.

PEOPLE   Help us, we beseech Thee, to keep the road
open for Him into our hearts.

LEADER   Most compassionate Father, send the Spirit of
Thy Son, this day, to all who sit in darkness within the
walled cities of their own sorrows or problems. May
they hear the song of rejoicing of those who love
Jesus.

PEOPLE   O Thou who has been made King and Lord of
glory, enter, we pray Thee, into our hearts.

Suggested Hymns "All Hail the Power of Jesus'
Name"; "All Glory, Laud, and Honor"; "Ride On!
Ride On in Majesty"; "Crown Him With Many
Crowns"

Suggested Scripture Readings

From the Psalms   24; 118
Old Testament Lesson   Zechariah 9:9–14; Malachi
3:1–12
New Testament Lesson   Matthew 21:1–17; Mark
11:1–11; Luke 19:28–40

Pastoral Prayer

O Lord of love, who on this day long ago entered the
rebellious city, confronting head-on the entrenched
evils; we are grateful that Thy Spirit is forever seeking
entrance into our world's life—as the impulse for fair-
ness—as the yearning to eliminate injustice and war—as
the self-giving spirit that bears other's burdens even to a
cross.

O Lord, give us responsive hearts and lasting devotion, lest we be found among those who speak well of
Thee when it is popular to do so, and then deny Thee
when the cost is great. Increase our conviction in Jesus,
we pray, so that we may be numbered among those who
bear in our hands the scars of the cross and rejoice in the
eternal triumphs, when every knee shall bow and every
tongue confess that Thou art the King of kings and Lord
of lords. *Amen.*

Offertory Sentence

"Take heed, and beware of all covetousness; for a
man's life does not consist in the abundance of his possessions" (Luke 12:15).

Offertory Prayer

O Christ, King of Life, who long ago asked for the use of a donkey to enter the city, grant that we may not withhold our possessions when Thou dost say, "I have need of it." Help us to crown Thee as the Master even in our giving for Thy Kingdom's sake. *Amen.*

Suggested Anthems "The King's Welcome" (Whitehead); "Hosanna to the Son of David" (Weelkes); "The Palms" (Faure)

Suggested Closing Hymn "All Hail the Power of Jesus' Name"; "Ride On! Ride On in Majesty"

Benediction

"Now may the Lord of peace himself give you peace at all times in all ways. The Lord be with you all" (2 Thessalonians 3:16).

MAUNDY THURSDAY COMMUNION

Calls to Worship

MINISTER "Christ, our paschal lamb, has been sacrificed. Let us, therefore, celebrate the festival, . . . with the unleavened bread of sincerity and truth" (1 Corinthians 5:6,7).

PEOPLE "Behold, the Lamb of God, who takes away the sin of the world!" (John 1:29).

or:

MINISTER   "Seek ye the Lord while he may be found, call ye upon him while he is near: Let the wicked forsake his way, and the unrighteous man his thoughts: and let him return unto the Lord, and he will have mercy upon him; and to our God, for he will abundantly pardon" (Isaiah 55:6,7 KJV).

PEOPLE   "Our help is in the name of the Lord, who made heaven and earth. . . . The Lord is nigh unto all them that call upon him, to all that call upon him in truth" (Psalms 124:8; 145:18 KJV).

MINISTER   "The Lord is merciful and gracious, slow to anger, and plenteous in mercy . . ." (*see* Psalms 86:15). "If we confess our sins, he is faithful and just, and will forgive our sins and cleanse us from all unrighteousness" (1 John 1:9).

PEOPLE   "Seeing that we have a great high priest, that is passed into the heavens, Jesus, the Son of God: let us therefore come boldly unto the throne of grace, that we may obtain mercy, and find grace to help in time of need" (*see* Hebrews 4:14,16).

Invocation

Lord Jesus Christ, who on this night long ago instituted the memorial supper, during which the betrayer was revealed; grant us the eyes of faith to discern Thy presence through the communion emblems. In Thy presence here, help us to see our own betrayals, so that we may be brought to repentance, lest we be a party to crucifying Thee anew. Breathe on us a spirit of humility and service, according to Your example in washing

Your disciples' feet. Speak to our hearts in the hallowed hush of this communion, that we may learn how to love Thee more worthily, O Christ our Lord. *Amen.*

Suggested Hymns "My Faith Looks Up to Thee"; "Here, O My Lord, I See Thee Face to Face"; "Bread of the World"; "Here at Thy Table Lord"; "When I Survey the Wondrous Cross"; " 'Tis Midnight, and on Olive's Brow"

Suggested Scripture Readings   Mark 14:17–26

Unison Prayer of Confession (MINISTER and PEOPLE)
For the sorrows which brought no softening of heart, for the chastenings which yielded no peaceable fruit of righteousness, for the rebukes of conscience which led to no amendment of life, have mercy upon us, O God, we humbly entreat Thee.

For the counsels of Thy Word we have known and not loved, for the Gospel of Thy Son we have believed and not obeyed, and for the leading of the spirit of truth we have acknowledged and not followed, have mercy upon us, O God, we humbly entreat Thee. *Amen.*

Communion Invitation
"And when the hour came, he sat at table, and the apostles with him. And he said to them, 'I have earnestly desired to eat this passover with you before I suffer; for I tell you I shall not eat it until it is fulfilled in the kingdom of God' " (Luke 22:14–16).

Words of Institution

"We have not a high priest who is unable to sympathize with our weaknesses, but one who in every respect has been tempted as we are, yet without sin. Let us then with confidence draw near to the throne of grace, that we may receive mercy and find grace to help in time of need" (Hebrews 4:15,16).

The Communion Participation

Suggested Anthem   "Thou Man of Grief, Remember Me" (Dare); or "He Shall Feed His Flock" (Handel)

Words of Assurance

"He was wounded for our transgressions, he was bruised for our iniquities; upon him was the chastisement that made us whole, and with his stripes we are healed" (Isaiah 53:5).

Closing Hymn   "Bread of the World"

Closing Prayer

"May the God of peace himself sanctify you wholly; and may your spirit and soul and body be kept sound and blameless at the coming of our Lord Jesus Christ" (1 Thessalonians 5:23).

GOOD FRIDAY

LEADER   "Is it nothing to you, all ye that pass by?"
PEOPLE   "Behold, and see if there be any sorrow like unto [His] sorrow" (Lamentations 1:12 KJV).

LEADER   "God commendeth his love toward us, in that, while we were yet sinners, Christ died for us" (Romans 5:8 KJV).

PEOPLE   "Behold the Lamb of God, who takes away the sin of the world!" (John 1:29).

or:

"He was wounded for our transgressions, he was bruised for our iniquities: the chastisement of our peace was upon him; and with his stripes we are healed" (Isaiah 53:5 KJV).

Hymns   "O Sacred Head, Now Wounded"; "Alas! And Did My Savior Bleed"

Invocation

Almighty God, our Father, in this hour of solemn remembrance, we acknowledge with sorrow and shame that our sins are such as sent our Lord to the cross. We come beseeching Thee mercifully to guide us in our meditations, supplications, and prayers and to dispose the minds and hearts of all men everywhere toward the attainment of everlasting salvation, through Jesus Christ. *Amen.*

Suggested Anthem   "Lamb of God" (Haydn); or "Crucifixion" (Stainer)

The First Word
Scripture Lesson   Luke 23:32–38
Suggested Hymn   "Jesus Calls Us O'er the Tumult"; or "O Come and Mourn With Me Awhile"

Prayer

Everloving and merciful Father, who art always more
ready to forgive than we are to repent, we remember this
day the suffering and death of our Lord Jesus Christ,
and confess to Thee our shame in the sins which crucified Him. Grant us grace that we may be reconciled to
Thee, through Thy Son and our Lord. *Amen.*

Meditation Starter   "The Word of Forgiveness"

This is one of the most comforting passages in all
the New Testament. It reveals the magnanimous spirit
of Jesus toward His persecutors in the midst of agony.
The burden of His prayer was for forgiveness for all
who had a part in His Crucifixion, but in particular
for those too ignorant to see what they were doing.
The remarkable nature of the prayer stands out, as
one considers the groups gathered around the cross.
Few protested. Some sorrowed, but they sorrowed
over the suffering Jesus endured; only Jesus was concerned over the tragedy of the souls who could so in-
differently afflict it. It wasn't the pain inflicted upon
Him that hurt so much as the stupidity and blindness.
They had become accustomed to cruelty, and accepted the uncaring system.

The Second Word
Scripture Lesson   Luke 23:39–43
Suggested Hymn   "O Jesus I Have Promised"; or "Into
the Woods My Master Went"
Prayer

O Thou who art love, look mercifully upon the

poor, the oppressed, and all who are victims of the suffering, injustice, and misery which stalk the earth. Fill our hearts with Christ's compassion and hasten the coming of Thy Kingdom of justice and salvation, through Jesus Christ, our Lord.

Meditation Starter "The Word of Salvation"

The Crucifixion scene is a study in contrasts. Nowhere is this more evident than in the case of the two thieves, for the cross that stood between them thrust them worlds apart. One damned by bitterness; the other saved by hope. One cynical; the other responsive. One railed on Christ for His impotence; the other blessed Him for His compassion. Faced the same agonies, yet one believed he saw the mercy and authority of God in Jesus.

The Third Word

Scripture Lesson   John 19:25–27

Suggested Hymn   "What a Friend We Have in Jesus"; or "Near the Cross Her Vigil Keeping"

Prayer

Our God and Our Father, our Friend and Companion; grant that all the bonds of love and friendship may be made stronger and sweeter through Jesus Christ, who in His mental agony was not unmindful of His mother's or His disciple's needs, nor our need of one another's love and His supreme love. *Amen.*

Meditation Starter   "The Word of Remembrance"

This is a deeply moving scene—the compassionate thoughtfulness of One in the midst of agony to show tender concern for His mother's care. Mary had never really understood her Son. She seems to have been bothered by doubts about her Sons actions and sanity. That is why Jesus commended His mother to John, rather than to His brothers and sisters. Mary needed an understanding heart. The Crucifixion was a terrible experience for her. Jesus was concerned for her soul. He wanted her to be protected by the warm fellowship of a loyal believing heart. John and Mary needed each other. The Church is our "Beloved Community."

The Fourth Word

Scripture Lesson   Mark 15:33–34
Suggested Hymn   "In the Hour of Trial"; or "Alone Thou Goest Forth, O Lord"; or " 'Tis Midnight, and on Olive's Brow"
Prayer

Almighty God, who are a tower of strength to all who put their trust in Thee, to whom all things in heaven and on earth at last must bow and surrender; even in our deepest agony help us to know and feel that we are not forsaken; that underneath are the everlasting arms; and that there is no other name under heaven given to man, in whom and through whom we may receive salvation—none but the name of Jesus Christ, Thy Son and our Lord. *Amen.*

Meditation Starter   "The Word of Loneliness"

No more poignant words have wrung from human lips than the quotation from the Twenty-second

Psalm: "My God, my God, why hast thou forsaken me?" His Kingship does not take away the desperate human emotion of desolation and abandonment that He felt. His humanity was responding, as well as His divinity. Have you ever thought how lonely God must be? How lonely Jesus must have been? He thought God would transform the cross into a triumph, yet there was no sign as yet. God restrained His power to interfere and left His love in Christ to stand alone, on its own, forcing evil's worst for all the world to see. Our hearts can trust Him who trusted love, faced death, and proved the victory.

The Fifth Word

Scripture Lesson   John 19:28,29

Suggested Hymn   "Beneath the Cross of Jesus"; or "Deep Were His Wounds"

Prayer

God our Heavenly Father, whose most dear Son found life not a bed of roses, but suffered pain, and entered not into glory before He was crucified; save us from believing that faith will keep us from troubles, and from becoming disillusioned or bitter if trouble does come. Grant that we, walking in the way of the cross, may find from Thee the strength to meet what we must, not in despair, but in peace with Thee and ourselves, through Jesus Christ. *Amen.*

Meditation Starter   "The Word of Suffering"

This is the only word from the cross referring to Jesus' physical suffering. Crucifixion was a most hor-

rible agony. No part of the body was free from pain.
There was an intolerable craving for water. We can't
explain away the suffering as the Gnostics did, saying
He "thirsted for God" or He "thirsted for human
souls." Suffering was *real* for Jesus. A great heresy of
the church today is not that we do not accept Jesus'
deity, but are superficial in accepting His humanity.
When God sought our salvation, He sought it through
a *human.* The cross is very precious; it declares that in
Him love had to suffer as man suffers. Only thus could
He save us, not as God from without, but as God
within us.

The Sixth Word
Scripture Lesson   John 19:30
Suggested Hymn   "When I Survey the Wondrous
Cross"; or "Go to Dark Gethsemane"
Prayer
    O God, we are thankful for the courage and devo-
tion of Jesus in facing the cross and enduring death
victoriously; thus fulfilling Thy mission for His life,
and the means of Thy redemption of the world. Increase in us true devotion to Thee, nourish us in faith,
and by Thy great mercy keep us steadfast, through
Jesus Christ our Lord. *Amen.*
Meditation Starter   "The Word of Triumph"
    What was finished? His agony? His ordeal? His
testing? His work as Messiah? His earthly destiny?
    One thing is certain—He had done what God had
laid upon Him to do. He had fulfilled His life's calling

in thirty-three years. The redemptive work was done; salvation's opportunity for all was accomplished; the cosmic struggle was over!

Even the cross had not forced Him to capitulate to evil forces. Love was loyal to the finish. Evil was impotent to overcome the qualities of love and faith that stood up before the powers of wickedness.

The Seventh Word

Scripture Lesson   Luke 23:44–49
Suggested Hymn   "In the Cross of Christ I Glory"
Prayer

O God our Father, beyond whose love and care we can never go; we thank Thee for the assurance that Thou art the Keeper of Life even after death. When we look upon Him who was wounded for our transgressions, we are brought low, and our pride is humbled. When we remember His spirit and faithfulness, even to death, we are inspired and, at the same time, stricken in conscience for our lack of courage and dedication. O God of mercy, uphold us by Thy strength, that in the end we may be accepted of Thee as faithful servants, in Jesus Christ our Savior. *Amen.*

Meditation Starter   "The Word of Reunion"

From one standpoint this might be the last desperate cry of a broken, defeated, dying spirit, giving up His dream. From another, it might be the final triumphant declaration of a confident faith putting His complete loyalty into the hands of the Father. There is a vast difference.

Jesus put His life into the hands of God unconditionally and let Him take Him through to the place where faith had to face the ultimate trial. It was not playacting. It was a terrifying experience. Christian discipleship calls for an adventure in love, which accepts suffering and frustration and commits it to God's hands, confident that He will use it and fulfill it.

Suggested Closing Hymns "What Wondrous Love Is This"; "Were You There When They Crucified My Lord?"

Benediction
". . . To him who loves us and has freed us from our sins by his blood and made us a kingdom, priests to his God and Father, to him be glory and dominion for ever and ever. Amen" (Revelation 1:5,6).

EASTER

Call to Worship
Christ is risen! He is risen, indeed! Hallelujah! The Lord God omnipotent reigns! To the King, immortal, invisible, the only God, be honor and glory, forever and ever! Come, let us worship God, and to Him let us pray.

Invocation
Everliving God, glorious is Thy name! Majestic is the Good News! Our life has been changed forever. Thy light of Easter dispels the darkness of our doubts. Thy power in love changes our reliance. Thy vindication of

Jesus reassures our faith. Hallelujah, praise Thy holy name.

or:

Righteous God, our Father; we come reverently to this place as worshipers, not as spectators; to bow before Thee, not to see or to be seen; to adorn ourselves inwardly with beauty, not to parade ourselves outwardly. May the words of our mouths and the meditations of our hearts be acceptable unto Thee, O Lord, our strength and Redeemer. *Amen.*

Suggested Scripture Readings

From the Psalms 16, 118

Old Testament Lessons Isaiah 25:1–9; Exodus 15:1–18

New Testament Lessons John 20:1–18; Colossians 3:1–11

Suggested Hymns "Christ the Lord Is Risen Today"; "Look, Ye Saints! The Sight Is Glorious"; "I Know That My Redeemer Lives"; "Thine Is the Glory"; "All Hail the Power of Jesus' Name"

Pastoral Prayer

Eternal God, Father of our Lord Jesus Christ, who turned the tragedy of evil of men into a triumph of faith and an assurance of love, who turned death into a glorious Resurrection and made the symbol of shame into a sign of triumph; we worship Thee. We thank Thee for the beauty of Jesus' life, the truth of His teaching, the nobility of His death, and the victory of His Resurrection.

We confess to Thee our broken promises, our self-centeredness, our desecration of the holy, our living as if there were no God, our absorption in the temporal as if there were no eternal. Have mercy upon us, merciful Father.

Illumine Thy eternal purpose and replenish with new hope all who are discouraged about the world, so sunshine may break through the clouds. Release those entombed in pride and hatred; surprise them with a resurrection of Thy love and joy in their hearts. Bless with Thy peace and assurance all who are ill. Protect in Thy love those who once shared life with us, but whose faces we see no more.

Arouse Thy church to a new sense of mission and revive Thy ways in the world through Easter's message of Jesus Christ, Lord Eternal. *Amen.*

Offertory Sentence

"Great is our Lord, and abundant in power; his understanding is beyond measure.... Sing to the Lord with thanksgiving.... and pay your vows to the Most High" (Psalms 147:5,7; 50:14). God is not unrighteous to forget your work and labor of love, which you have showed toward His name.

Offertory Prayer

God our Father, who has put at our disposal the power of money, influence, and personality; help us to use them as a channel of Thy purposes, so that Thy name may be known upon the earth and Thy saving power among all peoples, through Jesus Christ. *Amen.*

Suggested Anthem *Gloria* from *The Twelfth Mass* (Mozart); or, "Alleluia" (Thompson)

Suggested Closing Hymns "Rejoice, the Lord Is King"; "The Strife Is O'er"

Benedictions

"[To him who] will be made manifest at the proper time by the blessed and only Sovereign, the King of kings and Lord of lords, who alone has immortality and dwells in unapproachable light, whom no man has ever seen or can see. To him be honor and eternal dominion. Amen" (1 Timothy 6:15,16).

or:

"Now to him who is able to keep you from falling and to present you without blemish before the presence of his glory with rejoicing, to the only God, our Savior through Jesus Christ our Lord, be glory, majesty, dominion, and authority, before all time and now and for ever. Amen" (Jude 24,25).

Postludes "Lenten Postlude" (Kock); *Te Deum laudamus* (Claussmann)

19

EASTER SERVICE OF WORSHIP

THE RISEN LORD APPEARS

The Prelude   *Gloria* (Mozart)

The Choral Call

Call to Worship

MINISTER   "This is the day which the Lord has made; let us rejoice and be glad in it" (Psalms 118:24).

PEOPLE   "Christ being raised from the dead, dies no more; death has no more dominion over Him. The whole world's darkness is scattered." (*See* Romans 6:9.)

MINISTER   Rejoice in the Lord always, again I say, *Rejoice!* Let the angelic choirs of heaven now rejoice. Let the divine mysteries rejoice. Let all the earth rejoice. Let the church rejoice. Let every person here rejoice.

The Hymn of Joy   "Christ the Lord Is Risen Today"

Lighting of the Candles Symbolizing Christ Alive

THE RISEN LORD APPEARS
TO ONE IN SORROW

The Scripture Story   John 20:1, 11–18

The Prayer

Eternal God, our Father, we praise Thee for the joy that comes into our hearts on this Easter morn. As the risen Christ brought hope to ones in sorrow long ago, we thank Thee that He can also bring new hope to us. Lift us from the depths of sorrow and sadness, we pray, as we are ever mindful of His victory over death. As Thou hast turned the shadows of death into rays of morning light, wilt Thou illumine our spirits with hope of life eternal, through Jesus Christ our Lord.

Choral Amen

THE RISEN LORD APPEARS
TO ONE WHO DOUBTED

The Scripture Story   John 20:19–29

The Affirmation of Faith

LEADER As our spirits have weakened under the pressures of temptation and doubt, let us remind ourselves of the great beliefs of our faith.

LEADER AND PEOPLE We believe in the one God, Maker and Ruler of all things. Father of all men; the Source of all goodness and beauty, all truth and love.

We believe in Jesus Christ, God manifest in the

flesh, our Teacher, Example, and Redeemer, the Savior of the world.

We believe in the Holy Spirit, God present with us for guidance, for comfort, and for strength.

We believe in the forgiveness of sins, in the life of love and prayer, and in grace equal to every need.

We believe in the Word of God contained in the Old and New Testaments, as the sufficient rule both of faith and of practice.

We believe in the church as the fellowship for worship and for service of all who are united to the living Lord.

We believe in the Kingdom of God as the divine rule in human society; and in the brotherhood of man under the Fatherhood of God.

We believe in the final triumph of righteousness, and in the life everlasting. *Amen.*

THE RISEN LORD APPEARS TO THOSE WHO WERE DEFEATED

The Scripture Story   Luke 24:13–32

Hymn   "Look, Ye Saints! The Sight Is Glorious"

THE RISEN LORD APPEARS TO ONE WHO DENIED HIM

The Scripture Story   John 21:1,4,9,15–19

Gloria patri

The Presentation of Tithes and Offerings

Easter Anthem "I Know That My Redeemer Lives"

The Doxology and the Prayer of Dedication

THE RISEN LORD APPEARS
TO US IN THE SPIRIT

The Easter Sermon "Turning Scars Into Stars"

The Hymn of Triumph "Crown Him With Many Crowns"

Benediction

"Now may the God of peace who brought again from the dead our Lord Jesus, the great shepherd of the sheep, by the blood of the eternal covenant, equip you with everything good that you may do his will, working in you that which is pleasing in his sight, through Jesus Christ; to whom be glory for ever and ever. Amen" (Hebrews 13:20,21).

Postlude "Trumpet Triumphant in C" (Purcell) or "Lenten Postlude" (Kock)

20

PENTECOST

Calls to Worship
"Peter said to them, 'Repent, and be baptized every
one of you in the name of Jesus Christ for the forgiveness of your sins; and you shall receive the gift of the
Holy Spirit. . . . those who received his word were baptized, and there were added that day about three thousand souls. And they devoted themselves to the apostles'
teaching and fellowship, to the breaking of bread and
the prayers' " (Acts 2:38,41,42). This was the first Pentecost experience, and thus Christ's Church was born.
This we celebrate today.

or:

"You shall receive power when the Holy Spirit has
come upon you; and you shall be my witnesses in Jeru-
salem and in all Judea and Samaria and to the end of
the earth" (Acts 1:8).

Invocation
O God, who art known as Creator-Father, as Savior
Jesus Christ, and as resident Holy Spirit; look graciously
upon us assembled with one accord in one place to make
our prayers and to wait for Thy promise. By Thy mercy
renew in our longing hearts Thy Holy Gift, through
Jesus Christ our Lord. *Amen.*

Suggested Hymns   "Spirit of God, Descend Upon My Heart"; "Spirit of the Living God"; "Holy Spirit, Truth Divine"; "I Love Thy Kingdom, Lord"; "The Church's One Foundation"

Suggested Scriptures

From the Psalms   84; 145:1–3,18–21

Old Testament Lesson   Joel 2:21–32; Isaiah 61

New Testament Lesson   Acts 2:1–24; 1 Corinthians 14:1–12,18,19

Pastoral Prayer

Spirit of the Living God; breathe upon us Thy gracious power. Come to us as a mighty rushing wind, scattering our doubts, giving us warmth and gentleness, stirring our spirits to health, sweeping aside the fears that have held us captive.

O Lord, disturb our sleep, that suddenly we may find ourselves hungering for Thee, and for fellowship with all mankind. Come to us like a flame of fire to cleanse us from mental darkness and moral pollution.

Search deep to the core of our "self," that we may know Thee in business as well as in worship, in Jesus' name. *Amen.*

Offertory Sentence

If you then, who are evil, know how to give good gifts to your children, how much more will the Heavenly Father give the Holy Spirit to those who ask Him?

Offertory Prayer

Holy Spirit of God, give us a due sense of Thy greatness and mercy, that our hearts may be ever thankful,

that we may show forth Thy praise, not only with our
lips, but in our lives, by giving ourselves in Thy service,
and by walking righteously all our days, in Jesus' name.
Amen.

Suggested Anthem   "How Lovely Are the Messengers"
(Brahms)

Suggested Closing Hymns
"O Holy Spirit, Come to Me"; "Breathe on Me,
Breath of God"

Closing Prayer

> Spirit of the Living God,
> Fall afresh on me;
> Melt me, mould me,
> Fill me, use me.
> Spirit of the Living God,
> Fall afresh on me.
>
>   DANIEL IVERSON

or:

"Beloved, build yourselves up on your most holy
faith; pray in the Holy Spirit; keep yourselves
in the love of God; wait for the mercy of our Lord
Jesus Christ unto eternal life" (Jude 20,21).

21

WORLDWIDE COMMUNION SERVICE[8]

The Prelude

The Chimes

The Call to Worship

In every corner of the earth, North and South, East and West, people who love Christ and are a part of His body, meet in worship, fellowship, and service. From majestic cathedrals to thatch-roofed huts, from crowded house-churches to open-air services, in every tongue and of every race, Christians lift up their voices to "Our Father in Heaven." Come, dear friends, let us join the world company of Christ, as we worship and commune together.

THE PROCESSION OF NATIONAL FLAGS
AND CHRISTIAN FLAG

(REPRESENTATIVE *of continents may be flag bearers or youth may be dressed in appropriate costumes*)

The Unison Invocation Prayer

O God, our Heavenly Father, who so loved the world that you gave Your Son for all people; we are mindful of the unseen kinship which binds our hearts in Christian

115

love with all Your children. Lift us to new heights of
praise and deeper levels of understanding, as we worship
this day. Keep us sensitive to the bonds of Christian love
and discipline us to the Spirit and will of Jesus Christ
our Lord, in whose name we pray.

Choral Response

THE WORLD FELLOWSHIP OF THE CHURCH

The Scripture Readings
  Old Testament Psalms 133:1–3
  New Testament Matthew 26:26–29; Ephesians 2:4–6;
  Ephesians 4:3b; John 17:21

Greeting From the Continents (NARRATOR *and*
  REPRESENTATIVES *for churches of the continents*)
NARRATOR God created a vast beautiful world. On
  every continent today Christians will gather to have
  Holy Communion. Flags from many nations are on
  display in the chancel and throughout the church.

Australia and New Zealand
NARRATOR A "new" country of opportunity . . . new
  resorts and vacationland . . . koala bears and kan-
  garoos . . . bushmen . . . tennis excellence . . . Alan
  Walker, the Billy Graham of Australia . . . Australia,
  almost as big as the United States, not counting
  Alaska . . . and New Zealand, one thousand miles in
  length . . . rodeos . . . the Outback . . . aborigines.

The Greeting

REPRESENTATIVE   The Christians "Down Under" greet you in the name of Christ and join in Holy Communion.

Antarctica

NARRATOR   Two-thirds as large as North America . . . land and sea around the South Pole . . . icebergs . . . Ross Ice Shelf, four hundred miles long . . . Admiral Byrd and "Little America" . . . in prehistoric times, it may have had a climate like present-day California . . . currently eighty degrees below zero in the winter and hovering around zero in the summer.

The Greeting

REPRESENTATIVE   The Christians in Antarctica greet you, and in the name of Christ join in Holy Communion.

Africa

NARRATOR   Beautiful Victoria Falls . . . rich diamond mines and gold mines . . . a land ennobled by the great medical missionary work of Albert Schweitzer . . . the pioneer missionary outreach of David Livingstone . . . a continent where disciples have continued to let the light of Christ shine.

The Greeting

REPRESENTATIVE   The Christians in Africa greet you, and in the name of Christ join in Holy Communion.

Europe

NARRATOR   Colorful Europe . . . often called the birth-place of Western Civilization . . . Shakespeare . . . Byron . . . Keats . . . Parliament . . . flowers in Brussels . . . Versailles . . . windmills in Holland . . . The Black Forest . . . Bach . . . Beethoven . . . Chopin . . . Mozart . . . Raphael . . . Jungfrau . . . The Kremlin . . . Norwegian fjords . . . Dag Hammarskjold . . . The Vatican . . . John Knox . . . John Calvin . . . Martin Luther . . . John and Charles Wesley . . . Westminster Abbey . . . St. Mark's in Venice . . . Notre Dame . . . Saint Peter's.

The Greeting

REPRESENTATIVE   The Christians in Europe greet you, and in the name of Christ join in Holy Communion.

South America

NARRATOR   A land of contrasts—from revolutions and fear to the Christ of the Andes, a statue standing on the border of Chile and Argentina, which "represents peace between these countries," and the centrality of Jesus Christ to that peace . . . coffee . . . rubber.

The Greeting

REPRESENTATIVE   The Christians in South America greet you, and in the name of Christ join in Holy Communion.

North America

NARRATOR   A broad expanse from the frozen land of the Yukon, the Canadian wilderness, to the tip of Mexico . . . from the history of Plymouth Rock and

Jamestown to the Colorado Rockies and the orange groves of California ... the coal mines of West Virginia to the resorts on Padre Island ... automobiles in Detroit and cotton in Mississippi ... the Dallas Cowboys and the Toronto Maple Leafs ... Ralph Waldo Emerson and Mark Twain.

The Greeting

REPRESENTATIVE The Christians all over North America greet you, and in the name of Christ join in Holy Communion.

Asia

NARRATOR Enormous Asia ... overcrowded Asia ... rich ... poor ... starvation in the streets of Calcutta ... one of the Seven Wonders of the World, the ecstatically beautiful and architecturally proportioned Taj Mahal ... The Korean War ... The Vietnamese War ... Christians in the minority among Buddhists, Hindus, Shintoists ... yet an International Christian University in Japan ... a cathedral reopened in China ... masses of people ... the Lord's Supper being observed today.

The Greeting

REPRESENTATIVE The Christians of Asia greet you, and in Christ's name join in Holy Communion.

The Unison Affirmation (*congregation standing*)

This is my Father's world. It is a beautiful home for us, His children. It is a world of trees and flowers, mountains and lakes, food and energy. It is a world of living things, plants and animals, men and women, friends and loved ones. God so loved the world that He gave Jesus, His Son, to unify and redeem all creation. Whoever follows Him shall have joy and peace, and shall not perish but have eternal life. Praise be to God.

Gloria patri

The Sermon   "Our Oneness in Christ"

Hymn   "In Christ There Is No East or West"

THE TABLE OF COMMUNION
(Host—Jesus Christ)

The Invitation

This is the Lord's Table. He invites His followers of all churches to eat *The Bread of Life* and to drink the *Cup of Salvation.* In every continent of the world, Christians of all denominations and confessions will accept Christ's invitation to wholeness and to "eat and drink" in memory of Him.

Choral Anthem   "Let Us Break Bread Together" (COMMUNION DISTRIBUTORS *take their places about the table.*)

The Prayer for the Bread and Cup

Blessed be Thy name, O Lord our God! Through Thy Son's death and Resurrection, You have raised us from the depths into heavenly places, given us life out of death, brought us into freedom out of bondage, given us light and scattered the darkness of sin. Grant that as these emblems enter our bodies, we may accept Thy forgiveness, sense the unity of other followers of the Way, be filled with Thy Spirit, and present our bodies as living sacrifices to be used as You will, in Jesus' Kingdom. *Amen.*

The Words of Institution

"The bread which we break, is it not a participation in the body of Christ? Because there is one bread, we who are many are one body, for we all partake of the one bread."

"For by one Spirit we were all baptized into one body—Jews or Greeks, slaves or free—and all were made to drink of one Spirit" (1 Corinthians 10:16,17; 12:13).

The Joy of Sharing Communion

Organ Music "Come Now, Redeemer of Our Race" (Buxtehude)

The Words of Assurance

"So then you are no longer strangers and sojourners, but you are fellow citizens with the saints and members of the household of God, built upon the foundation of the apostles and prophets, Christ Jesus himself being the chief cornerstone" (Ephesians 2:19,20).

"By this is my Father glorified, that you bear much fruit, and so prove to be my disciples" (John 15:8).

OUR GIFTS TO CHRIST AND HIS CHURCH

Hymn   "We've a Story to Tell to the Nations"

The Opportunity to Share Presented
"God so loved the world that he gave his only Son
. . ." (John 3:16). Because He loves us, let us give Him
priority in our lives with our tithes and offerings, and
strengthen His Kingdom among all men.

The Offertory

Doxology

Prayer of Thanksgiving
Father of mankind, accept the gifts of our gratitude,
as we place them upon Thine altar for the ministry Thy
church can render, and as tokens of our renewed dedication to Thy Kingdom of love for all men. In Jesus' name,
who taught us to pray:

Unison Lord's Prayer

The Postlude

SECTION III

SERVICES SURROUNDING
THE FAMILY

An Abbreviated Marriage Ceremony . . . An Interdenominational Ceremony . . . Baby Blessing and Parent Dedication Service . . . The Service of Christian Baptism . . . Baptismal Liturgies (For Believer's Immersion Baptism; For Traditions Baptizing Infants) . . . Home Dedication . . . Fiftieth Wedding Anniversary Service

22

AN ABBREVIATED MARRIAGE CEREMONY

Friends, we are gathered here in the presence of God, to join together _____ and _____ in marriage. Let us remember that God has established marriage for the welfare and happiness of mankind. Our Savior declared that a man shall leave his father and mother and cleave to his wife. His apostles instructed those who enter into this relationship to cherish a mutual esteem and love, to bear with each other's infirmities and weaknesses; to comfort each other in sickness, trouble, and sorrow; to provide for each other in temporal things; to encourage one another in the things which pertain to God; and to live together in a sacred covenant of trust and peace.

Let us pray: God our Heavenly Father, whose favor we seek for every relationship; we present unto Thee this couple who desire to be married. As You love them, so may they love each other. By Thy Spirit, give them a warm heart for their new relationship; the gift of grace whereby they may enjoy the privileges, honorably fulfill the responsibilities, and patiently endure the trials; the gift of common sense and communication in meeting

problems. Deepen their union under Thy fatherly guidance and protection, through Jesus Christ. *Amen.*

To signify your willingness to make such a covenant,
and as a seal of the vows you are to make, will you join
your right hands?

PASTOR _____ , will you have
_____ to be your wedded wife, to live
together after God's ordinance in the holy estate of
marriage?

GROOM I, _____ , accept you
_____ as my wedded wife, to share in
the fulness of life, as long as we both shall live.

PASTOR _____ , will you have
_____ to be your wedded husband, to
live together after God's ordinance in the holy estate
of marriage?

BRIDE I _____ , accept you
_____ , as my wedded husband to
share in the fulness of life, as long as we both shall live.

PASTOR What symbol do you now exchange as an out-
ward sign of your love?

O God, may these rings ever signify the love of these
two—fashioned in circles without an ending, so may
their love be eternal; made of enduring and beautiful
substance, so may their love glow with increasing luster
through the years. Bless each that gives and each that
wears, that they may keep the bond of the holy covenant, in Christ's Spirit. *Amen.*

GROOM With this wedding ring, I pledge my love and
loyalty forever.

BRIDE   With this wedding ring, I pledge my love and loyalty forever. Wherever you go, I will go, and wherever you dwell, I will dwell.

GROOM   Your people shall be my people, and your God my God.

PASTOR   Since you, _____ and you, _____ have exchanged your vows, and in the presence of God, I, with the authority invested in me as a minister of Jesus Christ, pronounce you husband and wife.

Let us pray: The Lord fill you with all spiritual benediction and grace, that you may live together in the fullness of life.

May you have peace—
Not of the stagnant pool, but of deep waters, flowing.
May you have poise—
Not of the sheltered tree, but of the oak, deep rooted, storm strengthened, and free.
May you have power—
Not of fisted might, but of the quickened seed stretching toward infinite light. *Amen.*

(GROOM *salutes the* BRIDE *with a kiss. Couple turns, facing the congregation.*)

PASTOR   I present for your congratulations: Mr. and Mrs. _____.

23

AN INTERDENOMINATIONAL CEREMONY

(This service is designed for young people of different religious traditions such as Protestant and Roman Catholic, Episcopal and Free Church, as well as other denominations. It presumes participation by two clergymen, with the bride's minister as host.

The service therefore is designed to include portions familiar to most every Christian tradition—including Protestant, Roman Catholic, and Orthodox. An attempt has been made to couch the service in a contemporary flavor.)

Processional   "Greensleeves"

Call to Worship

HOST MINISTER   Friends, we are gathered together in the sight of God, within the presence of this company to join together _____ and _____ in holy matrimony. It is an honorable estate, instituted of God, and symbolizing the concern of the community of mankind in the covenant which they are now about to make.

"In the beginning God created the heavens and the earth.... Then God said, 'Let us make man in our image.' ... So God created man ... in the image of

God he created him; male and female he created them. . . . Then the LORD said, 'It is not good that man should be alone. . . . Therefore a man leaves his father and his mother and cleaves to his wife, and they become one flesh."

From the beginning, God blessed the marriage union.

Invocation

HOST MINISTER   O Lord, our Lord . . .

CONGREGATION   How excellent is Your name in all the earth.

HOST MINISTER   O Lord, hear my prayer . . .

CONGREGATION   And let my cry come to You.

HOST MINISTER   The Lord be with you . . .

CONGREGATION   And with your spirit.

HOST MINISTER   Let us pray. Direct, O Lord, all of our actions by Your inspiration. May every prayer and work of ours begin from You and be brought to completion, in Your holy name.

CONGREGATION   *Amen.*

Hymn (*optional*)   "Praise to the Lord, the Almighty" (*two verses*)

The Declaration of Intention

GUEST CLERGYMAN   From the dawn of human history, it has been customary for society to put the seal of public approval upon the union of man and woman. By the loving devotion and sacrifice of innumerable men and women through the long ages, this relationship has been purified and ennobled, until married love has become a center of clearest realization of the divine purpose in human life.

It is therefore not to be entered into inadvisedly or lightly, but discreetly and in the love of God.

In this holy estate, these two persons come now to be joined.

HOST CLERGYMAN   Who presents this bride in marriage?

FATHER OF BRIDE   Her mother and I do.

HOST CLERGYMAN   This union in which you are about to enter will influence your whole future. That future, with its joys and disappointments, successes and failures, pleasures and pains, is hidden from your eyes. Not knowing what is before you, you come now to take each other for better or for worse, for richer or for poorer, in sickness and in health, until death parts you.

HOST CLERGYMAN (*to* GROOM) _____ , will you have _____ to be your wedded wife, to live together after God's ordinance in the holy estate of matrimony, according to the holy rite of the Church of God?

GROOM   I will.

CLERGYMAN (*to* BRIDE) _____ , will you have _____ to be your wedded husband, to live together after God's ordinance in the holy estate of matrimony, according to the holy rite of the Church of God?

BRIDE   I will.

Unison Lord's Prayer

1 Corinthians 13:4-7 (*paraphrased*)

GUEST CLERGYMAN   Love is patient and kind; love is not jealous, or conceited, or proud; love is not ill-mannered, or selfish, or irritable ... love does not keep a record of wrongs; love is not happy with evil, but is happy with the truth. Love never gives up; its faith, hope, and patience never fail.

Sealing of the Marriage Bond

HOST MINISTER   Now, join your right hands and speak your vows.

GROOM   I _____, accept you _____, as my wedded wife, to share in the fullness of living, as long as we both shall live, because I love you very much.

BRIDE   I _____, accept you _____, as my wedded husband, to share in the fullness of living, as long as we both shall live, because I love you very much.

Blessing of the Wedding Rings

HOST MINISTER   As a symbol of your constant and abiding love and of being joined together in holy marriage, you will give and receive a ring. (*Rings given to the* CLERGYMAN.)

HOST MINISTER   The Lord be with you.

CONGREGATION   And with your spirit.

MINISTER   Let us pray. Bless, O Lord, these rings so that those who wear them, keeping faith with each

other in unbroken loyalty, may ever remain constant
in mutual love and be at peace according to Your will
and Spirit.

CONGREGATION   *Amen.*

HOST MINISTER   Now that you have sealed your wedding covenant, give these wedding rings to each other.

GROOM   _____, take and wear this ring as a
sign of our marriage vows.

BRIDE   _____, take and wear this ring as a
sign of our marriage vows.

Confirmation of the Marriage Bonds

HOST MINISTER   By the authority of the church, I ratify
and bless the bond of marriage you have contracted.
In the name of the Father, and of the Son, and of the
Holy Spirit.

CONGREGATION   *Amen.*

HOST MINISTER   I will call upon all of you, here present, to be witnesses of this holy union, which I have
now blessed. "Man must not separate what God has
joined together."

CONGREGATION   What, therefore, God has joined together, let no man put asunder.

GUEST CLERGYMAN   Let us kneel in prayer. Eternal
God, whose grace promises all things, strengthen
_____ and _____ with the gift of
Your Holy Spirit, that they may fulfill the vows they
have taken. Help them to keep faithful to each other
and to You. Fill them with such love and joy, so that
when misunderstandings, irritations, and temptations

occur, they may be quick to forgive, generous in patience, and dependably strong. Grant them fullness of years, so that they may reap the harvest of the good life. Guide them by the counsel of Your Word. When their earthly life is complete, give to them Your eternal dominion in the unity of peace, forever and forever.

CONGREGATION *Amen.*

Unison Prayer (BOTH MINISTERS *and* MARRIED COUPLE)

Lord, make us instruments of Your peace,
Where there is hatred, let us sow love;
Where there is injury, pardon;
Where there is doubt, faith;
Where there is despair; hope;
Where there is darkness, light;
Where there is sadness, joy.

O Divine Master, grant that we may not so much seek to be consoled, as to console; to be understood as to understand; to be loved as to love.

For it is in giving that we receive; it is in pardoning that we are pardoned; and it is in dying that we are born to eternal life.

Benediction

GUEST CLERGYMAN May the peace of God dwell in your hearts and in your home. May you have true friends to stand by you, both in joy and in sorrow. May you be strong in grace and love, now and forever. *Amen.*

Symbolic Memory Candlelighting   (BRIDE *and* GROOM
   *take outside lighted candles of a three-pronged
   candelabrum and together light the center candle, then
   extinguish the two outside candles.*)

HOST MINISTER   "It is not good that man should be
   alone.... Therefore a man leaves his father and his
   mother and cleaves to his wife, and they shall be one
   flesh" (Genesis 2:18,24). As two lights are now
   blended into one, so two lives are blended into one.
      May you be one in name, one in aim, and one in
   happy destiny together.

(GROOM *salutes the* BRIDE *with a kiss. Couple turns, facing the congregation.*)

HOST   MINISTER I   present   Mr.   and   Mrs.
   _____.

Recessional   "Trumpet Voluntary in D" (Purcell)

24

BABY BLESSING AND
PARENT DEDICATION SERVICE

Explanation

_____, you have brought this child
_____, into this sacred place of worship for
God's anointment and your dedication of yourselves to
rear the child in the Christian way of life.

It has scriptural precedent, for Jesus our Lord, as a baby, was brought by Mary and Joseph to the Temple, where the prophet, Simeon, took Him in his arms, blessed Him according to their custom, and they dedicated themselves to the sacred responsibility.

This is a service of thanksgiving to God for the joy and hope that has come into your lives by the presence of this child. It is recognition of God as the Giver of Life and an affirmation that all children are His. It is a reconsecration of yourselves.

The love of a home will help determine (his) future characteristics. God will enrich (his) life, if you will keep the doors of your own lives open to God.

Do you dedicate your child to God? ANSWER: We do.

Do you promise to give your child the best that you have learned of the ways and love of your Heavenly Father, so that (he) may grow into the love and nurture and admonition of the Lord? ANSWER: We do.

Pastoral Prayer

Heavenly Father, gracious and merciful, we thank Thee that Thou has given these the privilege of parenthood, and has blessed their home with this little life.

Bless this child, O Lord, with strength of body, soundness of mind, and health of soul.

Help these parents to keep Christian values, to develop Christian priorities, and to walk in the paths committed to faith, truth, justice, and righteousness so that this child may grow toward Thee. Grant them patience

and wisdom, good judgment and balance for this de-
manding task, in the name of Jesus Christ. (PASTOR
takes BABY *in arms.*)

This is _____, born_____. The
paternal grandparents are _____. The mater-
nal grandparents are _____.

Blessing Prayer

"The Lord bless you and keep you: the Lord make his
face to shine upon you, and be gracious to you: the Lord
lift up his countenance upon you, and give you peace"
[throughout your life. *Amen.*] (Numbers 6:24–26).

25

THE SERVICE OF CHRISTIAN BAPTISM

Gathering Music

Call to Worship

MINISTER   "O taste and see that the Lord is good!"

RESPONSE   "Happy is the man who takes refuge in
him!" (Psalms 34:8).

UNISON   "Blessed are those who wash their robes, that
they may have the right to the tree of life and that
they may enter the city by the gates" (Revelation
22:14).

Opening Hymn "We Bless the Name of Christ, the Lord" or "Living for Jesus" or "I Can Hear My Savior Calling"

Invocation

Most merciful Father, as the Holy Spirit came upon our Lord and Savior Jesus Christ at His baptism, so may Your presence be realized by all of us participating here in this ordinance of baptism, either as candidate or member of the community of faith, so that our faith may be made more alive in Jesus Christ. *Amen.*

Reading the Corporate Memories of The Community of Faith

Matthew 3:13–17; John 3:5; Romans 6:3–11

Praise Hymn *Gloria patri*

Homily "The Spiritual Meanings in Baptism"

The Affirmation of Faith (*in unison or each sentence repeated after minister.*)

I believe in the living God, the Father of mankind, who creates and sustains the universe by His power and His love.

I believe in Jesus Christ, the Man of Nazareth, because of His words and work, His way with others, His use of suffering, His conquest of death.

I know what human life ought to be and what God is like.

I believe that the Spirit of God is present with us, now and always, and can be experienced in prayer, in forgiveness, in the Word, the sacraments, the fellowship of the church, and in all we do. *Amen.*

Prayer

O Lord, accept and fill with Thy Spirit this one now to
be baptized, in the name of Jesus Christ. *Amen.*

The Baptism (*See alternate liturgies in chapter 26
recorded for immersion baptism or for infants*)

Hymn "O Happy Day" or "Come Holy Spirit, Dove
Divine" or "Savior, Thy Dying Love"

Benediction

"Now may the God of peace, who brought again from
the dead our Lord Jesus, the great shepherd of the sheep,
by the blood of the eternal covenant, equip you with
everything good that you may do his will, working in
you that which is pleasing in his sight, through Jesus
Christ . . ." (Hebrews 13:20,21).

26

BAPTISMAL LITURGIES

FOR BELIEVER'S IMMERSION BAPTISM

Minister's Statement

The divine authority for baptism comes from Jesus,
who said, "All authority in heaven and on earth has
been given to me. Go therefore and make disciples of all

nations, baptizing them in the name of the Father and of the Son and of the Holy Spirit" (Matthew 28:18,19). We witness here this symbolic ceremony of obedience to the Lordship of Christ; the forgiveness of sin and cleansing of life; identification with the saving acts of God in the death; burial and Resurrection of Christ; and the beginning of a new life in a new family with new allegiances and a new name—Christian.

The Baptism Prayer

Gracious God, our Father and the Father of our Lord, Jesus Christ, who has made us to become Your children through Him; bless _____ as (he) is baptized, that (his) body may become a temple for Your Spirit and (his) life shall increasingly attain to the measure of the stature of Jesus Christ. Renew us spiritually, as we share in the joyous portrayal of redemptive love, and cause us to be good members of Your family in Christ. *Amen.*

The Baptism

MINISTER *to* CANDIDATE   God is witness to what you are doing. Center your thoughts on Him, as I pronounce the baptismal formula.

The Baptismal Formula

_____(*name*) upon your confession of faith in the Lord Jesus Christ, and now in obedience to His will, you are baptized in the name of the Father, the Son, and the Holy Spirit. *Amen.*

The Baptismal Blessing

Let your heart rejoice in the salvation of God (*see* Psalms 13:5); (*or*) "May the joy of Jesus Christ our Lord, make full your joy" (*see* John 15:11); (*or*) The Lord bless you and keep you.

THIS LITURGY IS FOR TRADITIONS BAPTIZING INFANTS
(*adapted from a worship service book published by Congregational Christian Churches, USA*)

Minister's Statement

You have brought your child here desiring for him Christian Baptism, which is the sacrament of entrance into the love and care of the Church of Christ. This is a service of thanksgiving, as we offer to God the gratitude of our hearts for the hope and happiness which comes into our lives by the presence of a child. It is a recognition of God as the Giver of Life and a testimony that all children are His. This service, also, is one of dedication and consecration; the dedication of your child to God; and your own consecration to fidelity that you may give your child the best that you have learned of the ways and love of your Heavenly Father.

Do you promise to make known the goodwill and love of the Heavenly Father that your child may grow into the love and nurture of the Lord?

RESPONSE   I (*or we*) do.

MINISTER Do you promise that you will teach this child the principles of our Christian religion, and that you will pray with (him) and for (him)?

RESPONSE I (*or we*) do.

Prayer

O Lord, grant to these parents the grace to perform that which they have promised before You. And sanctify with Your Spirit this child now to be committed in Christian faith to You. *Amen.*

The Baptism

By what name shall this child be called? (PARENT *gives name.*)

_____, I baptize you in the name of the Father, and of the Son, and of the Holy Spirit. *Amen.*

This child is now received into the love and care of the church in the good hope that hereafter (he) may never be ashamed to confess the faith of Christ, but may be kept steadfast in His love, and continue to be Christ's faithful servant until his life's end. May you to whom has been committed this trust of teaching and training this child in discipleship, be wise, loving, devout, loyal and obedient to God's will.

Solo "Take My Life and Let It Be"

27

HOME DEDICATION SERVICE

(*May begin with an Open House and social hour. The service itself may be conducted by the* PASTOR *and* FAMILY MEMBERS.)

Opening Statement

FATHER *or* MOTHER   On behalf of our family we are happy to welcome you to our home. We consider that you are a part of our larger family. Because our family is Christ-centered, we wanted to dedicate our home, and to have you share with us. We want you to know our minister, _____, whom we have invited to lead the service.

MINISTER   A London magazine one time asked its subscribers to define a home. Out of nearly one thousand replies, six were selected as the best definitions of a home:

- *Home*—a world of strife shut out, a world of love shut in.
- *Home*—a place where the small are great, and the great are small.
- *Home*—the father's kingdom, the mother's world, and the child's paradise.
- *Home*—the place where we grumble the most and are treated the best.

- *Home*—the center of our affection, 'round which our heart's best wishes twine.
- *Home*—the place where our stomach gets three square meals a day and our hearts a thousand. A home is all this, but it is a great deal more.[9]

Candlelighting Ritual (FAMILY MEMBERS *will light the candles.*)

MINISTER   We believe a home has a personality. It is not the wood and stone that make a home, but the folks who live within—the way they live together; the way they live with their neighbors; the way they live with God. This constitutes the personality of the house.

_____ will light one of the candles representing *personality*.

MINISTER   We believe that the keystone which holds a home together is the spirit of true love, a love that deepens and broadens through the years.

_____ will light a candle representing *love*.

MINISTER   We believe that wisdom and common sense should help true love govern a home. Love alone may often be blind, but wisdom and common sense furnish two good eyes that help love find the right pathway.

_____ will light a candle representing *wisdom* and *common sense*.

MINISTER   We believe that a home should be honest. It is not a place for sham or make-believe living. Genuineness and sincerity should be practiced by those within and seen by those without.

_____ will light a candle representing *hon-esty*.

MINISTER   We believe that home should be a place in which peace and harmony touch all lives that step over the threshold. Harsh words, uncontrolled temper, sullen dispositions are unwelcomed guests.

_____ will light a candle representing *harmony*.

MINISTER   We believe that the home is the nursery of heaven, one of the departments in the school of life. It is the home where we first learn the art of living together.

_____ will light a candle representing *learning*.

MINISTER   We believe that the home can be a temple made holy by the Spirit of the living God, and blessed by the teachings of Jesus Christ. With that presence, all the storms from without will not destroy the home, and a warm glow will burn within, even as Jesus indicated.

_____ will light a candle representing God's presence.

Scripture Readings

Matthew 7:24–27 (*by the* FATHER)

1 Corinthians 13, paraphrased (*by the* MOTHER)

My home may be made beautiful by the wealth of the world, but if it has not love, it is only an empty shell. My home may be the rendezvous of the witty and the meeting place of the wise, but if it has not love, it is only a noisy house. My home may distribute its welcome to men of every estate; my home may toil for the betterment of all mankind, but if it has not love, its influence will soon vanish.

The spirit of a true home is very patient, very kind; it knows no jealousy, makes no parade, gives itself no airs, is never rude, never selfish, never irritated, never resentful. It is never gladdened when sorrow comes to another home, is made happy by goodness, always slow to talk with others about the intimacies of the home, always eager to believe the best, always hopeful, always enduring. The home will never disappear. As for civilizations, they will be superseded; as for knowledge, it will grow out of date; as for institutions, they will close. For we only know a little now and we can see only dimly into the future, but when the spirit of a true home rules the affairs of this earth, then will be established the perfect Kingdom of God. Thus faith and hope and love last on forever in our homes, these three, but the greatest of all is love.[10]

The Ceremony of Dedication

PASTOR   As a place where marriage is held in honor, with husband and wife living faithfully together ...

FAMILY *and* FRIENDS   We dedicate this home.

PASTOR   As a place where family members may be rich in understanding, courteous and kind, bearing one another's burdens ...

FAMILY *and* FRIENDS   We dedicate this home.

PASTOR   As a place where each family member may

find rest when he or she is weary, refreshment when hungry, encouragement when depressed, and acceptance when hurting . . .

FAMILY *and* FRIENDS   We dedicate this home.

PASTOR   As a place of hospitality to the neighbor, and beacon light to the lost and wayward . . .

FAMILY *and* FRIENDS   We dedicate this home.

Pastoral Prayer

God our Father, of whom the whole family in heaven and on earth is named; we pray Thy blessing upon the family of this home. Embrace this home in the undying bonds of love, through Jesus Christ, our Lord. *Amen.*

Solo   "Bless This House"

28

FIFTIETH WEDDING ANNIVERSARY SERVICE

Statement of Explanation   (*one of* SONS *or* DAUGHTERS)

We welcome family and friends to this Fiftieth Wedding Anniversary of our parents, Mr. and Mrs. _____. The church and a strong personal faith have been a great part of our parents' lives.

Therefore, we invite you to participate in a few moments of worship to celebrate this occasion.

Instrumental Prelude "Now Thank We All Our God"; "Thine Is the Glory"; "O Perfect Love"

Sentences of Worship

Unto God be the glory on this occasion and on every occasion of our lives. "Rejoice in the Lord always, again I will say, Rejoice" (Philippians 4:4).

Hymn "Love Divine, All Love Excelling"

> Love divine, all love excelling,
> Joy of heaven, to earth come down;
> Fix in us Thy humble dwelling,
> All Thy faithful mercies crown!
> Jesus, Thou art all compassion,
> Pure, unbounded love Thou art;
> Visit us with Thy salvation,
> Enter every trembling heart.
>
> Come, Almighty to deliver,
> Let us all Thy life receive;
> Suddenly return, and never,
> Nevermore Thy temples leave.
> Thee we would be always blessing,
> Serve Thee as Thy hosts above,
> Pray, and praise Thee without ceasing,
> Glory in Thy perfect love.

CHARLES WESLEY

God's Word in Scripture: 1 Corinthians 13 (LB)

Prayer

Heavenly Father, who designed the pattern of the family for the experiences of life from the cradle to the grave, and made it the image-relationship for the Heavenly Kingdom; we thank you for _____ who celebrate fifty years of married life together. We praise You for the ties that bind their hearts in Christian love, and for the kind providence that has sustained them in health and happiness. We are grateful for their maturity in sharing hard times as well as good, in transcending the irritations and difficulties that beset all marriages in one way or another, and for the family which they have reared.

Bless them, dear God, with continued health. We pray for their children and grandchildren that from this example each might learn new possibilities for happiness, patience to endure and to understand, and renewed devotion to the marriage vows. Settle all of us happily in our families; we pray in the name of Jesus Christ in whom is concord and peace. *Amen.*

Meditation: "Love Never Ends"

When the apostle Paul said, "Love never ends," he meant love never disappears, never falls down on the job, never gives up.

The happy and enduring marriage is based on more than "romantic love"; it requires Christian love, which promises not to fail nor give up. Christian love promises to love the other person under all conditions, even when the going is roughest, when one must "give" rather than just "get" from the relationship. It promises to love "for better, for worse, for richer, for poorer, in sickness and in health."

In a sense, Christian love is the only gift we have that will not come to an end—for love is of God, and God is love.

"Love bears all things; believes all things; hopes all things" even when the grounds for hope are dim. Nothing gets love down—no disillusionment, no disappointments, no adverse circumstances, no height nor depth, nor any creature. True love will never end.

Prophecies will be made, fulfilled and pass away—not so love. Eloquent speaking and religious fads will come and go—but love will not. Knowledge today becomes obsolete tomorrow, as more perfect understanding does away with the imperfect—but the need for love is never out of date.

Love is the only thing that abides. All else fades away. Our riches will pass into other hands when we die. Fame, position, and possessions fade with the passing stream of the "not yet, through the now, to the no more." All of them fade away, but love does not. We lose other things; love is never lost.

Love is, therefore, the clue to immortality. It binds the life here with the life hereafter, and assures us that we shall meet our loved ones again.

Elizabeth Barrett Browning felt this way about her husband, which is expressed so beautifully in her love sonnet:

How do I love thee? Let me count the ways.
I love thee to the depth and breadth and height
My soul can reach, when feeling out of sight
For the ends of Being and ideal Grace.
I love thee to the level of everyday's
Most quiet need, by sun and candle-light.
I love thee freely, as men strive for Right,
I love thee purely, as they turn from Praise.
I love thee with the passion put to use
In my old griefs, and with my childhood's faith.
I love thee with a love I seemed to lose
With my lost saints—and I love thee with the breath,
Smiles, tears, of all my life!—and, if God choose,
I shall but love thee better after death.

Moment of Quiet Prayer and Commitment

Renewal of Wedding Vows

(*The traditional wedding vows will be recited. Other couples are invited to renew their marriage vows. Please face one another and repeat the phrases after the* MINISTER, *to your companion.*)

MINISTER   Please say to your wife: I _____,
take you _____, to be my wedded wife, to
have and to hold from this day forward, for better for
worse, for richer for poorer, in sickness and in health,
to love and to cherish, till death do us part, according
to God's holy ordinance.

(WIVES *repeat the same vows to* HUSBANDS.)

MINISTER   Let us pray:
O God, unite us now by faith with all these friends

and loved ones who have blessed our lives. Accept the rededication of Your servants to their marriage vows. For the years ahead, make plain the path, and abide with us all. Amid the changes of this mortal life, help us to fix our hope in You, where true joys are to be found. *Amen.*

Closing Hymn "O Love That Wilt Not Let Me Go" (*sing or read*)

> O love that wilt not let me go,
> I rest my weary soul in Thee;
> I give Thee back the life I owe,
> That in Thine ocean depths its flow
> May richer, fuller be.
>
> O Light that followest all my way,
> I yield my flickering torch to Thee;
> My heart restores its borrowed ray,
> That in Thy sunshine's blaze its day
> May brighter, fairer be.
>
> GEORGE MATHESON

SECTION IV

EVENTS OF COMMUNITY AND BEYOND

Prayers for Community Occasions (Mayor's Installation; Annual Chamber of Commerce Dinner; A Chamber of Commerce Meeting; Community Museum; Political Rally; Luncheon Prayer for the Rehabilitation Center; Civic Club Prayers; Commencement Prayer) . . . A Community Service of Thanksgiving . . . Community Brotherhood Service (Litany of Brotherhood) . . . Bilingual Convention Material . . . Convention Communion Service (Worship Sentences for An Area Meeting) . . . Community Easter Sunrise Service.

29

PRAYERS FOR COMMUNITY OCCASIONS

MAYOR'S INSTALLATION

O Lord of goodness and peace, in a time when our nation struggles for its survival against irresponsible outbursts of greed, violence, and turmoil, we bow humbly seeking divine guidance.

You watched over the Pilgrims, as they drew up the Mayflower Compact; over those who drafted and signed the Declaration of Independence. You have inspired many to work for justice, and liberty and happiness for all. So guide us all to work constructively with our problems, as co-workers for Your Kingdom.

We bow in gratitude for our heritage, acknowledging others have labored and we enter into their labors.

We stand in appreciation for those who have served here.

As we open a new chapter in this city's life, we are grateful for a life to live, and a life to give.

Bless our new City Mayor with the spirit and wisdom, leadership and patience to sustain harmony amid progress, and to blend diversity into unity.

Bless the Councilmen, newly and past-elected, to

work for right, that each may exercise self-control and prepare adequately for responsible service, for the sake of this city and her citizens, in Thy holy name. *Amen.*

ANNUAL CHAMBER OF COMMERCE DINNER

Eternal God, unto whom all creation owes its existence, who art the source of meaning, freedom, and love; we stand reverently before Thee, grateful for our nation, for our life in it, for the resources of the community, and for our common endeavors for its progress.

In a particular way, we thank Thee for those who have served the Chamber of Commerce this year.

O Lord, bless to our enjoyment the fellowship and program of this evening, and this food to our health and service, we pray in Thy holy name. *Amen.*

A CHAMBER OF COMMERCE MEETING

One truth we have learned, O God—that things in this world seldom stay the same for long. Each day brings new opportunities, new demands, new problems.

Today in this meeting, O Lord, we are replanning, reorganizing, redreaming for our city and its people's needs. Grant to all of us patience to listen to new ideas, flexibility to be open to new approaches, sympathy for those who protest, grace to honor the decisions intended for our common good, freedom from past animosity, and wisdom to know what to do and how to do it. One thing we do recognize, O Lord, the constancy of Thy will, and our never-changing purpose in life. So, save us from wavering—we pray in Your name, who changes not. *Amen.*

COMMUNITY MUSEUM

God of history and freedom, we thank Thee for the Community Museum which reminds us of our political heritage and the processes of democracy which have given us freedom. Help us, O God, to become more responsible, knowledgeable citizens. To that end we rededicate ourselves this day, in Thy name. *Amen.*

POLITICAL RALLY

God of all history, whose providence brought this nation into existence—

We thank Thee for a free society, for the privilege and responsibility of electing our own representatives and leaders, including the Chief Executive.

For the men who have served as President of our country for the past two hundred plus years, we are humbly grateful. We pray for the one who serves us now, and others who will serve in the future. Sustain our government, we pray. Cleanse us of all unrighteousness.

We come here, symbolically, to rededicate ourselves to the principles of free government under God, in whose name we pray. *Amen.*

LUNCHEON PRAYER FOR THE
REHABILITATION CENTER

O Thou of compassion, whose love was demonstrated by Jesus, who wept with the lonely and assisted the unfortunate, we bow in thoughtful gratitude.

By Thy wisdom, the provisions of earth sustain our bodies. By Thy mercy, struggling hearts are made strong. By Thy love lodged in human hearts, pain is removed and handicaps mended through this Center.

Bless, we pray, this Board in its decisions; the employees in their service; and the patients to which this program is dedicated.

In Thy holy name. *Amen.*

CIVIC CLUB PRAYERS

1

Our Heavenly Maker, as we close our eyes, we think of all the varied blessings which we have taken too much for granted: a green world to live in; pure air to breathe; a home to share; family to care; friends to cherish; a work to do; and a service to render; the tranquility of a starlit night; a leaf floating on quiet water; sunshine after rain; the peace of Thy indwelling Spirit.

O Lord, dispel our low moods with a consciousness of how lucky we are to be alive and to be free. *Amen.*

2

Father of all: Thou has made us one nation out of many people. Amid our diversity of race, class, and background, unite us in a common love of freedom. Bless this club in its efforts to provide fellowship and promote understanding among men, for Thy Kingdom's sake. *Amen.*

3

Bless O Lord, this food to our strength, and us to unselfish service, in the developing community of brotherhood, in Thy name we pray. *Amen.*

4

God of Righteousness; in these days when evil hands soil the sacred, when righteousness is betrayed in high places, and when crime threatens the nations, grant strength and courage to every leader and every group that contributes to building firm convictions, pure hearts, and moral integrity. O Lord, may their number ever increase for the healing of the nations, in Thy holy name. *Amen.*

COMMENCEMENT PRAYER

Eternal God, whose kind providence has led us to this glad day, we pause to express gratitude.

We give Thee thanks for each graduate, and the high achievement which this day symbolizes. We lift up our thanks for the hopes and sacrifices of their families, the devoted efforts of their teachers, and the abiding confidence of the community.

May tonight be truly a commencement into larger journeys of learning and higher levels of experience. May each be equipped to meet life triumphantly. Guide them in their decisive decision. May they have the courage to love the pure, to seek the truth, and to fight for right, even though that may mean sacrifice, weariness, and unpopularity. May they continue to grow in godliness, until at last they are prepared to graduate into life eternal with Thee. *Amen.*

30

A COMMUNITY SERVICE OF THANKSGIVING

The Preparation for Worship   Musical Prelude

The Call to Worship

LEADER   "O Lord, how manifold are thy works! In wisdom hast thou made them all; the earth is full of thy creatures" (Psalms 104:24).

PEOPLE "Bless the Lord, O my soul, and forget not all his benefits" (103:2).

LEADER "I will pay my vows to the Lord in the presence of all his people, in the courts of the house of the Lord" (116:18,19).

PEOPLE "I will offer to thee the sacrifice of thanksgiving and call on the name of the Lord" (116:17).

The Invocation (*in unison*)

Almighty God, our Heavenly Father, the fountain of all goodness, who satisfies the needs of every living thing; we give Thee thanks that Thy kind mercy has brought us through the circuit of another year, and that the provision of seedtime and harvest has been experienced once again. We praise Thee that the year has been crowned with mercy and that Thou has bestowed upon us the abundant fruits of earth. Grant us grace that we may receive them gratefully and use them worthily for our own needs, for the relief of the less fortunate, and for Thy glory. Teach us to remember that it is not by bread alone man lives; and lead us to feed upon the true bread of life, according to Thy Holy Word. *Amen.*

Hymn of Thanks "For the Beauty of the Earth" or "From All That Dwell Below the Skies"

The Reading From the Old Testament Psalms 65 or 103 or Psalms 107:1–22

The Prayer of Thanksgiving

Eternal God, our Heavenly Father, by whose Spirit all things were brought into existence; by whose wisdom human life was formed; by whose grace we have a life to live and to use to magnify Thee and Thy will; we worship Thee. Lord, we have come here to express our thankfulness. For the work of Thy Spirit in the struggle for freedom and unity throughout the ages, from which heritage we have benefited, we thank Thee, O Lord. For the growing reverence for womanhood and opportunities for all Thy children regardless of class or color, and for the fuller life for all, we thank Thee, O Lord. For the dreams of Thy Kingdom of love and brotherhood which never cease to haunt and lure the world through men of goodwill, we thank Thee, O Lord.

Forgive us, Merciful Father; for our absorption in the trivial; for the temptations of our affluent culture that erode our faith and compromise our loyalty; for the moral obtuseness that accepts evil with no indignation; for the self-pride which blinds us from our inadequacies; for our divisive spirits and self-centeredness, we plead Thy mercy. *Amen.*

Hymn "Now Thank We All Our God" or "America, the Beautiful"

The Reading From the New Testament Luke 17:11–19.

Gloria patri

The Invitation to the Offering

The Anthem

Presentation of Tithes and Offerings

Doxology and Fourth Verse of "America"

The Prayer of Dedication

LEADER   Almighty God, Creator and Sustainer of all, Giver of every good and perfect gift; for the joy of seedtime and the riches of harvest ...

PEOPLE   We give Thee thanks, O God.

LEADER   For divine love that blesses our lives and speaks to our souls, reconciling us to Thee and to our fellowman ...

PEOPLE   We give Thee thanks, O God.

LEADER   Help us that our shops and factories, our homes and businesses, our bodies, minds, and strength may be used as a sacred trust from Thee ...

PEOPLE   We beseech Thee, O God.

UNISON   That we may be good stewards of all these blessings, and that we may so share our bounty with those in need across the world so as to cause all lands to break forth into songs of thanksgiving; we dedicate our offerings and ourselves to Thee, O God.

The Sermon   "Thanks—To Whom? For What? How?"

Hymn   "Come, Ye Thankful People, Come"

The Benediction
Now may you be given:
    A pure heart, that you may see God;
    A humble heart, that you may hear God;
    A loving heart, that you may serve God;
    A faithful heart, that you may abide in God.

The Postlude

31

COMMUNITY BROTHERHOOD SERVICE

(*For persons of all races, religions, ages, backgrounds*)

Prelude Music

Call to Worship

LEADER "Behold, how good and pleasant it is when brothers dwell in unity!" (Psalms 133:1).

PEOPLE "He made from one every nation of men to live on all the face of the earth" (Acts 17:26).

LEADER "So then you are no longer strangers and [foreigners] but you are fellow citizens with the saints and members of the household of God" (Ephesians 2:19).

PEOPLE "In him we live and move and have our being" (Acts 17:28).

LEADER "He is our peace, who has made us both one, and has broken down the dividing wall of hostility" (Ephesians 2:14).

PEOPLE "I looked, and behold, a great multitude ... from every nation ... and peoples and tongues ... clothed in white robes, with palm branches in their hands ... saying,

ALL "Blessing and glory and wisdom and thanksgiving be to our God forever and ever! Amen" (Revelation 7:9,12).

Invocation

O God, who has made us one in our need of Thee and of each other; we worship Thee as our common Heavenly Father. Grant us a fuller realization of our brotherhood. Allay all racial, social, and creedal prejudices and bitterness by establishing in us a sense of equity in all our doings, so that we may live in peace and concord through the Holy Spirit. *Amen.*

Hymn "All People That on Earth Do Dwell" or "There's a Wideness in God's Mercy"

Scripture Readings Romans 12:3–17; 1 Corinthians 12:12–26.

Prayer

O God, the Father of Grace, have mercy upon us and all men for blindness to truth and bitterness of spirit. Free our minds from intolerance and our hands from violence. Instruct and empower us to do Thy will. By Thy Holy Spirit, enlighten us, and make us compassionate and long-suffering. Enlarge our sympathies; broaden our trust; lengthen the paths of justice and true fellowship. Deliver all men from the bondage of hate and fear until Thy Kingdom comes on earth as it is in heaven. *Amen.*

Anthem "Where Cross the Crowded Ways of Life" or "All From the Same Clay"

Offertory With Doxology

Sermon

Hymn   "Rise Up, O Men Of God"

Benediction   "Litany of Brotherhood"

LEADER   Lord of all beings, we praise Thee for Thy kind providence, which has led us to this "Melting Pot" of the world which we call home.

PEOPLE   We thank Thee, O Lord, for this land where the oppressed have found liberty, the forgotten have found opportunity, and where the sons and daughters of toil have risen to positions of influence.

LEADER   We praise Thee, O Lord, that Thou has given to each race its own gifts and to each tongue its own message, and to each creed its own contribution.

PEOPLE   We thank Thee, Father of all mankind, that we have all been called to the high and holy task of perfecting Thy purposes which are yet unfulfilled.

LEADER   Good Lord, deliver us from the pride of race, or station, or creed which blinds us to the needs of others and to the kinship with all Thy children, and with Thee.

PEOPLE   Forgive us, Merciful Father, for doors we shut to the helpless, and to the seekers of opportunity, and to those who are different from us.

UNISON   We humbly beseech Thee, O Lord, that through renewed minds and amended deeds, we may so perfect our relationships with all sorts and conditions of people that Thy Way may be known upon the earth and Thy saving health among all nations.

So may it be.

32

BILINGUAL CONVENTION MATERIAL

(*Any combination of languages could be used in this service, depending on the locale of the gathering.*)

Sentences of Worship (*in Spanish and English*)

1

FIRST LEADER (*in English*) "Worship the Lord in holy array; ascribe to the Lord the glory due His name; for great is the Lord; and greatly to be praised." (*See* Psalms 29:2.)

CONGREGACIÓN (*en español*)
"Codicia y aun ardientemente desea mi alma los atrios de Jehová; mi corazón y mi carne cantan al Dios vivo" (Salmos 84:2).

LÍDER SEGUNDO (*en español*)
"Bienaventurados los que tienen hambre y sed de

justicia, porque ellos serán saciados" (Mateo 4:6).

PEOPLE

(*in English*)

"Satisfy us ... with thy steadfast love, that we may rejoice and be glad all our days" (Psalms 90:14).

2

LEADERS

(*in both languages*)

Dear Friends! Let us love one another, for love comes from God.

LÍDER

(*en ambos idiomas*)

Estimados Amigos! Amémonos el uno al otro, porque el amor viene de Dios.

ENGLISH SPEAKING

We love because God first loved us.

LOS DE HABLA ESPAÑOLA

Si alguno dice, "Yo amo a Dios," y aborrece a su hermano, el tal es mentiroso.

LEADERS

(*in both languages*)

For he cannot love God whom he has not seen, if he does not love his

	brother, whom he has seen.
LÍDER	*(en ambos idiomas)*
	Porque él no puede amar a Dios a quien no ha visto, si no ama a su hermano a quien ha visto.
ENGLISH SPEAKING	This, then, is the command that Christ gave us.
LOS DE HABLA ESPAÑOLA	El que ama a Dios ha de amar a su hermano también.
UNISON	*(in both languages)*
	O Divine Master, grant that we may not so much seek to be consoled as to console; to be understood as to understand; to be loved as to love—in Jesus' Spirit. *Amen.*
EN UNISO	*(en ambos idiomas)*
	Oh, Divino Maestro, concedenos que no busquemos ser consolados sino consolar; no ser comprendidos sino comprender; no tanto ser amados como amar, en el Espíritu de Jesús. *Amén.*

3

LEADER	We are here to celebrate life in Christ! Now is the time to come to the Father who creates us, to sing to the Lord who frees us, to pray with the Spirit who fills us.
LÍDER	Estamos aquí para celebrar vida en Cristo! Ahora es el momento para venir al Padre quien nos créo, para cantar al Señor quien nos libró, para orar con el Espíritu Santo que nos llena.
PEOPLE	Yes, now is the time to celebrate.
CONGREGACIÓN	Sí, ahora es el momento para celebrar.
LEADER	Let us invite the whole world to join us in praising God.
LÍDER	Invitemos a todo el mundo a unirse con nosotros para alabar a Dios.
PEOPLE	We invite the happy people and the sad people.

CONGREGACIÓN	Invitemos a la gente alegre y a la gente triste.
LEADER	We invite the haves and have nots, the employed and the poor, the white and the black, the brown and the red.
LÍDER	Invitemos a los que tienen y a los que no tienen, a los que trabajan y a los pobres, a los blancos y a los negros, a los morenos y a los de piel roja.
PEOPLE	We invite the Asians and the Europeans, the Latin Americans and the North Americans to know our joy in the Lord.
CONGREGACIÓN	Invitamos a los Asiáticos, y a los Europeos, a los Latinoamericanos y a los Norteamericanos; que conozcan nuestro gozo en el Señor.
UNISON	Praise be to Thee, O God, from whom come all the blessings of life in Jesus Christ. *Amen.*

EN UNISO

Alabanzas a tí oh Dios, de quien vienen todas las bendiciones de vida en Jesucristo. *Amén.*

4

FIRST LEADER

(*in English*)
We have come here
   in the name of the Father who made us
   in the name of the Son who makes us free
   in the name of the Spirit who makes us one.

LÍDER SEGUNDO

(*en español*)
Adoremos a Dios el Padre; Dios el Hijo; Dios el Espíritu Santo.

ENGLISH SPEAKING

While we may have different origins, ages, opinions, or occupations, yet we greet each other in the name of Jesus Christ.

LOS DE HABLA ESPAÑOLA

Porque Cristo nos une por medio de su llamada hacernos su pueblo. ¡Y porque El ama, nosotros nos podemos amar el uno al otro!

ENGLISH SPEAKING

Thus, we gather as a community of faith, the church, and recognize our common relationship through God's Son.

LOS DE HABLA ESPAÑOLA

Alabemos a Dios por haber hecho posible esto, y nos hechamos la carga de compartir su amor y su unidad con el resto del mundo en necesidad.

5

FIRST LEADER

(in English)
The grass withers, the flowers fade; but the word of God will stand forever.

LÍDER SEGUNDO

(en español)
Lámpara es a mis pies tu palabra, y lumbre a mi camino.

UNISON

(in both languages)
Open my eyes, that I may behold wondrous things out of thy law.... Make me understand the way of Thy precepts and I will meditate on Thy wondrous works.... Teach me,

EN UNÍSONO

O Lord, the way of Thy statutes; and I will keep it to the end. Give me understanding, that I may keep Thy law and observe it with my whole heart (Psalms 119:18,27,33,34). (*en ambos idiomas*)

Abre mis ojos y miraré las maravillas de tu ley. Hazme entender el camino de tus mandamientos y hablaré de tus maravillas. Enséñame, Oh, Jehová, el camino de tus estatutos, y los guardaré hasta el fin. Dáme entendimiento y guardaré tu ley; y la observaré de todo corazón (Salmos 119:18,27,33,34).

Unison Affirmation of Faith

(CONGREGATION *please stand. All who speak* SPANISH, *repeat the first phrase in unison; then all who speak* ENGLISH, *repeat next in unison.*)

Afirmacion de fe en unísono

(*La* CONGREGACIÓN *en pie. Los que hablan* ESPAÑOL, *leerán la primera frase en voz alta; despues los que hablan* INGLÉS *repetirán la frase en voz alta.*)

ESPAÑOL

Creemos en Dios, el
Espíritu Eterno, el Padre
de nuestro Señor Jesu-
cristo y nuestro Padre, y
damos testimonio a sus
hechos.

ENGLISH

He calls the worlds into
being, creates man in His
own image and sets before
him the ways of life and
death.

ESPAÑOL

El busca, en santo amor, a
salvar a todo pueblo de la
perdición y el pecado.

ENGLISH

He judges men and na-
tions by His righteous
will, declared through
prophets and apostles.

ESPAÑOL

En Jesucristo, hombre de
Nazaret, nuestro crucifi-
cado y resucitado Señor.

ENGLISH

He has come to us and
shared our common lot,
conquering sin and death,
and reconciling the world
to Himself.

ESPAÑOL

El nos otorga el Espíritu
Santo creando y reno-
vando la Iglesia de Jesu-
cristo, atando en un con-

venio a los fieles de todas edades, todas lenguas y todas razas.

ENGLISH

He calls us into His church, to accept the cost and joy of discipleship, to be His servants in the service of man, to proclaim the Gospel to all the world and resist the powers of evil, to share in Christ's baptism and eat at His table, to join Him in His passion and victory.

UNISON

He promises to all who trust Him, forgiveness of sins and fullness of grace, courage in the struggle for justice and peace, His presence in trial, and rejoicing and eternal life in His Kingdom which has no end. Blessing and honor, glory and power be unto Him.

EN UNISO

El promete a todos los que confían en el perdón de todos pecados y la plenitud y llenura de la gracia, valor en la lucha para la

justicia y la paz, su pre-
sencia en tribulación y re-
gocijo y vida eterna en su
Reino que no tiene fin.
Bendiciones   y   honor,
gloria y poder sean con
El.

33

CONVENTION COMMUNION SERVICE[12]
(for Regional or National Assembly)

Gathering Music

Processional Medley "We're Marching to Zion";
"Forward Through the Ages"

Call to Celebration

LEADER   Celebration is the mood of today's service.
Cry out for joy for what God has done in Christ!

PEOPLE   Amen! Amen! Amen!

LEADER   "You are a chosen people. God's own people.
Once you were no people, but now you are God's
people. Once you had not received mercy, but now
you have received mercy." *(See* 1 Peter 2:9,10) Clap
your hands for joy!

PEOPLE   *(clap their hands)*

LEADER   Let us pray:

Father of the new humanity in Christ, we humble ourselves in thankfulness, for the knowledge of Your presence and salvation. Grant that we might worship You with genuine hearts, and adequately prepare to partake of the family meal.

PEOPLE   We seek Your presence, Holy Father.

LEADER   Let our love for each other become genuine and strong; let us know that where there is love, You are present also.

PEOPLE   We seek to experience Your love, loving Father.

LEADER   Grant that Your love might enliven all of our relationships, so that we may know that Your church is present here.

PEOPLE   We seek to be your church, Forgiving Father, in Jesus' name. *Amen.*

Choral Response   *Gloria patri*

CELEBRATING AS GOD'S FAMILY

INTERPRETER ONE   "The Redeemed Family of God"
    Scripture Basis   Ephesians 2:19; 1 Peter 2:9,10.

Hymn   "In Christ There Is No East or West"

Prayer of Thanksgiving   *(Standing)*
    To be accepted into Your family, O God, is great! To be a part of this historic people, O God, is wonderful! To

be called to a mission of love is exciting! We come asking for nothing but a thankful spirit, in Jesus' name.
Amen.

CONFESSING OUR BROKENNESS

INTERPRETER TWO   "The Shameful Divisions in the
    Family"
    Scripture Basis   John 17:9–23.

Unison Confession Prayer   (WORSHIPERS *may kneel or
    remain seated, bowed in head to indicate remorse*)
    Let us pray:
    O God, we regret the splintered condition of Your
church. How can the world become community, when
we can't even be? We fullheartedly admit that we have
done and said many wrong things that have hurt the
church. We admit that we have neglected many opportunities to do loving things. Now we would turn away
from these sins. Father, be merciful to us. Please forgive
us. Turn us from our foolish ways, fill us with love and a
desire to serve Thee all our days. In Jesus' name. *Amen.*

Hymn   (*standing*) "Father Almighty, Bless Us With
    Thy Blessing" or, "Dear Lord and Father of
    Mankind"

Assurance of Pardon
    Hear the Good News: "If one is in Christ, he becomes
a new person altogether. The past is finished and gone.
Everything is fresh and new. Now you are no longer

strangers to God and foreigners to heaven, but you are members of God's very own family, citizens of God's country, and you belong in God's household with every other Christian" (Ephesians 2:19 *paraphrased*)

Gesture of Reconciliation   (*Persons embrace, head over one shoulder then the other, whispering* "God forgives us.")

LOVING ONE ANOTHER

Anthem   "Joshua Fit the Battle of Jericho" or "God Is Here—Let's Celebrate!"
INTERPRETER THREE   "The Walls Are Crumbling"
   Scripture Basis   Ephesians 2:13–22; 4:1–6

Hymn   "They'll Know We Are Christians by Our Love"

Offering to Express Fraternal Love

Litany on Church Unity[13]
LEADER   And Jesus said, "Thou art Peter, and upon this rock I will build my church."
PEOPLE   "And the gates of hell will not prevail against it" (Matthew 16:18 KJV).
LEADER   Because I love little country churches, hid among elms and birches; crying babes in arms, preachers unalarmed . . .
PEOPLE   I love Thy Kingdom, Lord, the house of Thine abode.

LEADER   I love city churches—inner-city churches, pointing ever to past accomplishments; yearning, hoping for a better day . . .

PEOPLE   The church our Blessed Redeemer saved with His own precious blood.

LEADER   I love black churches, with solid preaching, rousing music, handclapping, endless rounds of *Amens* and *Hallelujahs* . . .

PEOPLE   I love Thy church, O God; Her walls before Thee stand.

LEADER   I love churches—stately spires with traditional crosses pointing heavenward; odors of incense and candles burning . . .

PEOPLE   Dear as the apple of Thine eye, and graven on Thy hand.

LEADER   I love mission churches in mushrooming new areas at home or deep in the bowels of Africa, Asia— telling of Christ, often making little headway . . .

PEOPLE   For her my tears shall fall; for her my prayers ascend.

LEADER   I love house churches—people seated on carpeted floors, coffee cups rattling; with the sincere seeking and searching out new ways . . .

PEOPLE   To her my cares and toils be given, till toils and cares shall end.

LEADER   I love Quaker churches—a respite from much talking with periods of deep meditation; an occasional head nodding; Holy Spirit moving . . .

PEOPLE   Beyond my highest joy I prize her heavenly ways.

LEADER   I love the old-time churches—members clutching well-worn Bibles . . .

PEOPLE   Her sweet communion, solemn vows, her hymns of love and praise.

LEADER   I love institutional churches, now under attack; assembling baskets for the needy, attending wedding receptions, preaching Christ . . .

PEOPLE   Jesus, Thou Friend Divine, our Savior and our King!

LEADER   I love problem churches—old as the New Testament and as new as the last church council meeting, seeking improvement but often failing . . .

PEOPLE   Thy hand from every snare and foe shall great deliverance bring.

LEADER   I love suburban churches, somewhat sophisticated; well organized; services and activities programmed to meet every need . . .

PEOPLE   Sure as Thy truth shall last, to Zion shall be given.

LEADER   I love all churches with endless "hypocrites" included and all manner of faults, mistakes; yet, ever heeding Christ in attempted mission . . .

PEOPLE   The brightest glories earth can yield, and brighter bliss of heaven.

LEADER   "And all who believed were together and had all things in common" (Acts 43:44).

PEOPLE   And the Lord added to His church through the country church, the city church, the black church, the mission church, the house church, the Quaker church, the old-time church, the institutional church, the problem church, the suburban church, all churches—those that were being saved.

REALIZING OUR ONENESS

INTERPRETER FOUR   "One In Christ"
Scripture Basis   Colossians 1

Words of Institution

I hold in my hands a loaf of bread. I look at it . . . and see the fellowship of man . . . for throughout the ages, the eating of bread together says, "We are one body. No one here is stranger or alien." I look at this bread—and see in it the common life in which we are fulfilled. For the labor of many makes it available to the one. In this bread I see human dignity—work is the gift of oneself to the whole of which one is part.

I see in it the invisible life of Jesus Christ which sustains all people . . . no one can keep on being, apart from life's ever-renewing.

I look at this bread . . . and remember a broken body; to give hope, to give life!

So we are at the beginning of a miracle . . . this bread becomes personal life; becomes the deeds of people.

This cup is the new agreement between God and you that has been established and set in motion by Christ's love.

THE GREAT THANKSGIVING

Partake (*Each one serves his neighbor the loaf, then the cup.*)

Anthem "Let Us Break Bread Together"

Words of Assurance (*when Communion is finished*)
Isn't it heavenly? This is a foretaste to the Heavenly Kingdom—a world without end.

Unison Lord's Prayer (*paraphrased*)
Our Father, may all men come to respect and to love You. May You rule in every person and in all of life. Give us, day by day, the things of life we need. Forgive us our sins, for we forgive everyone who has done us wrong. Let nothing test us beyond our strength. Save us from our weakness. For Yours is the authority and the power and the glory, forever. *Amen.*

Passing of the Peace (*started by each section leader*)
"Brother _____ (or Sister) _____ may the love and peace of God be with you."

Hymn "Blest Be the Tie That Binds"

WORSHIP SENTENCES
FOR AN AREA MEETING

LEADER   This is a day which the Lord has made.
PEOPLE   This is a special day given to us by God, a day

never lived before by any man. Let us praise God for the gift.

LEADER   This is a time for Christians to come together in joyous praise.

PEOPLE   Let us celebrate together with our brothers and sisters of the _____ Area, the gift of life and joy in the body of Christ.

LEADER   This is a time for prayer and meditation.

PEOPLE   Let us come together to remember who we are, as children of God and disciples of Jesus.

LEADER   This is a time to learn.

PEOPLE   Let us have ears to hear, that we may receive a new word from God.

LEADER   This is a time to dream dreams.

PEOPLE   Let us have eyes to see new horizons and the potential that God has placed before us.

LEADER   This is a time for fellowship.

PEOPLE   Let us deepen our relationships and learn to be God's co-workers in love with all about us.

LEADER   This is a time for rededication.

PEOPLE   Let us give ourselves to Him who can make us new people in Christ.

34

COMMUNITY EASTER SUNRISE SERVICE
CELEBRATING EASTER'S ASSURANCE

Prelude Music "Trumpet Tune in C" (Purcell—*trumpets, timpani and so forth*)

Morning Hymn "Christ the Lord Is Risen Today" or "Thine Is the Glory"

The Celebration Antiphonal

MINISTER God has altered the human outlook forever! He has confirmed the best in humanity by His Resurrection. He has defeated the enemies of life. *Hallelujah!*

RESPONSE He has vindicated righteousness over evil, love over hate, and life over death. *Hallelujah!*

CHOIR "Hallelujah!" (*portion from* "The Hallelujah Chorus")

MINISTER God has given assurance to all men, in that He raised Jesus from the dead!

RESPONSE We are no longer tossed to and fro. We know "whom we have believed." We rejoice with unutterably great joy. *Hallelujah!*

CHOIR "Hallelujah!" (*portion from* "The Hallelujah Chorus")

Invocation *(may be in unison)*

Almighty, Everlasting God, Source of our life and Vindicator of Jesus Christ, our Lord; we lift our thoughts and emotions in praise and thanksgiving for the Easter event. Now we are assured that stronger than the evil which crucified Jesus is Your might. Stronger than the darkness of death is Your merciful power and plan.)Beyond the shattered hopes of Calvary, You have caused the world to sing, to hope, and to pray. Hallelujah!

CHOIR   "Hallelujah!" *(portion from* "The Hallelujah Chorus")

Congregational Hymn: "Look Ye Saints, the Sight Is Glorious" or "In the Garden"

Reading of the Easter Hope   *(from The Living Bible)*
From the Old Testament: Isaiah 25:1–8; or Psalms 16.
From the New Testament: John 20:1–18; Luke 24:1–12; 1 Corinthians 15:1–8, 35–44.

Easter Prayer

Like sunrise breaking the darkness of night, is Your vindication of Jesus to us, O God.

We had suspected that it made no difference how we lived—it would all end the same way. We had assumed the evil and powerful people had the last word in human destiny. We had been disheartened, discouraged, beaten, often disillusioned, because truth seemed always to get crucified while the evil, ill-mannered, and morally loose got all the breaks. Now, O God, into the gloom of despondency has come this reassurance, this delivering, hopeful word,

Speak this day the words of hope needed to every confused and gloomy soul. To the lonely, give assurance of Christ's empathy and companionship. To the downcast, give a transfusion of hope and joy. To the indifferent, give a shock that will awaken attention and captivate energy. To the lethargic church, grant a renewal of spirit, a cleansing of hypocrisy, and an understanding of mission to spread the Gospel of victory and to claim new territory for Christ. To a fearful, sin-sick world, give a clear hearing of the Easter message.

We remember those who once stood by us and shared our joys and sorrows, whose hands have been upon ours, but who are now a part of the great host of the invisible. Grant to us the continued inspiration of their lives and the anticipation of reunion.

From this sacred place of worship, send us out again, renewed, exalted, ennobled, empowered by the assurance that death is defeated, and that the greatest purpose in life is to serve Your will, in the name of Jesus Christ our Lord. *Amen.*

Anthem   "The Hallelujah Chorus"

Sermon   "Turning Sunsets Into Sunrises"

Dedication Hymn   "Crown Him With Many Crowns"

Dismissal

Now in the light of God's eternity, go forth to live for Him, with Him, and in His Spirit, until the day ends, the morning dawns, and God receives you into His eternal fellowship.

Benediction

To You, O God, be given respect and honor, obedience and love, both now and forever.

Silent Recessional

SOURCE NOTES

1. G. Edwin Osborne, *Christian Worship: A Service Book* (Saint Louis: Christian Board of Publication, 1953) page 137. Used by permission.
2. *Ibid.,* page 138. Used by permission.
3. Adapted from service used at Central Christian Church, Enid, Oklahoma, September, 1979. Dr. Lloyd Lambert, minister.
4. Darrell Faires, "What in the World Is the Meaning of This?" *Songs 'n Celebrae,* © Copyright 1971 by Darrell Faires. Used by permission.
5. Author unknown. Reprint from Christian Art Bulletin B12478 (Anderson, Indiana: Warner Press 1963).
6. Adapted from "Christmas Beatitudes," author unknown.
7. Author unknown. Reprint from Christian Art Bulletin B4279, Warner Brother Press, Inc.
8. Adapted from service by James Stoner, Minister, Central Christian Church, Austin, Texas.
9. Charles M. Crowe, *Sermons for Special Days* (New York: Pierce and Smith, 1951) page 246.
10. Robert W. Burns, "My Home," *Worship Services,* Charles L. Wallis, editor (New York: Harper Brothers, 1954) p. 269.
11. Materials written by author, used in Regional Assembly, Christian Churches of the Southwest, 1978.
12. Prepared by author. Used in World Convention Churches of Christ, Mexico City, August 4, 1974.
13. Raymond Gaylord, *World Call,* March, 1972. Used by permission of the author.

Index